Common Core
High School:
Geometry

**CCSS Test Review for the
Common Core State Standards Initiative**

Dear Future Exam Success Story:

Congratulations on your purchase of our study guide. Our goal in writing our study guide was to cover the content on the test, as well as provide insight into typical test taking mistakes and how to overcome them.

Standardized tests are a key component of being successful, which only increases the importance of doing well in the high-pressure high-stakes environment of test day. How well you do on this test will have a significant impact on your future, and we have the research and practical advice to help you execute on test day.

The product you're reading now is designed to exploit weaknesses in the test itself, and help you avoid the most common errors test takers frequently make.

How to use this study guide

We don't want to waste your time. Our study guide is fast-paced and fluff-free. We suggest going through it a number of times, as repetition is an important part of learning new information and concepts.

First, read through the study guide completely to get a feel for the content and organization. Read the general success strategies first, and then proceed to the content sections. Each tip has been carefully selected for its effectiveness.

Second, read through the study guide again, and take notes in the margins and highlight those sections where you may have a particular weakness.

Finally, bring the manual with you on test day and study it before the exam begins.

Your success is our success

We would be delighted to hear about your success. Send us an email and tell us your story. Thanks for your business and we wish you continued success.

Sincerely,

Mometrix Test Preparation Team

Need more help? Check out our flashcards at: http://MometrixFlashcards.com/CCSS

TABLE OF CONTENTS

Top 15 Test Taking Tips

1. Know the test directions, duration, topics, question types, how many questions
2. Setup a flexible study schedule at least 3-4 weeks before test day
3. Study during the time of day you are most alert, relaxed, and stress free
4. Maximize your learning style; visual learner use visual study aids, auditory learner use auditory study aids
5. Focus on your weakest knowledge base
6. Find a study partner to review with and help clarify questions
7. Practice, practice, practice
8. Get a good night's sleep; don't try to cram the night before the test
9. Eat a well balanced meal
10. Wear comfortable, loose fitting, layered clothing; prepare for it to be either cold or hot during the test
11. Eliminate the obviously wrong answer choices, then guess the first remaining choice
12. Pace yourself; don't rush, but keep working and move on if you get stuck
13. Maintain a positive attitude even if the test is going poorly
14. Keep your first answer unless you are positive it is wrong
15. Check your work, don't make a careless mistake

Congruence

Point and line

A point is a specific location and is used to help understand and define all other concepts in geometry. A point is denoted by a single capital letter, such as point P.

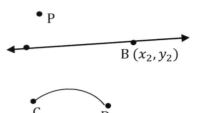

A line is a straight continuous set of points and usually denoted by two points in that set. For instance, $\overleftrightarrow{AB}$ is the line which passes through points A and B.

The distance along a line, or the distance between two points on a line, can be measured using a ruler. If the two points are located on the Cartesian plane, the distance can be found using the distance formula: $d = \sqrt{(x_2 - x_1)^2 + (y_2 - y_1)^2}$.

The distance around a circular arc, or the distance along a circle between two points, can be measured using a piece of string (to follow the shape of the circle) and then a ruler. The distance can also be found by finding the portion of the circle's circumference represented by the arc.

Angle, circle, perpendicular lines, parallel lines and line segment

Angle – The set of points which are part of two lines that intersect at a specific point. An angle is made up of two "half lines" called rays that begin at the shared point, called the vertex, and extend away from that point. An angle can be denoted simply by the angle's vertex ($\angle A$ or $\sphericalangle A$) or by three points: one from one ray, the point of intersection, and one from the second ray ($\angle BAC$ or $\sphericalangle BAC$).

Circle – A continuous set of points which are all equidistant from a separate point called the center. A circle usually shares the same label as its center: circle P with center at point P.

Perpendicular lines – Two lines which intersect at one specific point and create four 90° angles. Notation: $\overleftrightarrow{DE} \perp \overleftrightarrow{EF}$ when lines DE and EF intersect and form right angles at point E.

Parallel lines – Two lines which do not share any points and never intersect. Notation: $\overleftrightarrow{GH} \parallel \overleftrightarrow{IJ}$.

Line segment – The section of a line that is between two specific points on that line, usually denoted by two points: $\overline{KL}$.

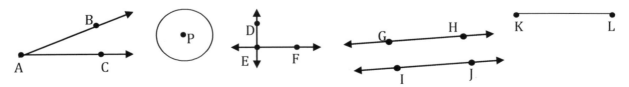

Rotation, center of rotation, and angle of rotation

A rotation is a transformation that turns a figure around a point called the center of rotation, which can lie anywhere in the plane. If a line is drawn from a point on a figure to the center of rotation, and another line is drawn from the center to the rotated image of that point, the angle between the two lines is the angle of rotation. The vertex of the angle of rotation is the center of rotation.

Reflection over a line and reflection in a point

A reflection of a figure over a line (a "flip") creates a congruent image that is the same distance from the line as the original figure but on the opposite side. The line of reflection is the perpendicular bisector of any line segment drawn from a point on the original figure to its reflected image (unless the point and its reflected image happen to be the same point, which happens when a figure is reflected over one of its own sides).

A reflection of a figure in a point is the same as the rotation of the figure 180° about that point. The image of the figure is congruent to the original figure. The point of reflection is the midpoint of a line segment which connects a point in the figure to its image (unless the point and its reflected image happen to be the same point, which happens when a figure is reflected in one of its own points).

Translation

A translation is a transformation which slides a figure from one position in the plane to another position in the plane. The original figure and the translated figure have the same size, shape, and orientation.

Transforming a given figure using rotation, reflection, and translation

To rotate a given figure: 1. Identify the point of rotation. 2. Using tracing paper, geometry software, or by approximation, recreate the figure at a new location around the point of rotation.

To reflect a given figure: 1. Identify the line of reflection. 2. By folding the paper, using geometry software, or by approximation, recreate the image at a new location on the other side of the line of reflection.

To translate a given figure: 1. Identify the new location. 2. Using graph paper, geometry software, or by approximation, recreate the figure in the new location. If using graph paper, make a chart of the x- and y-values to keep track of the coordinates of all critical points.

Identifying what transformation was used when given a figure and its transformed image

To identify that a figure has been rotated, look for evidence that the figure is still face-up, but has changed its orientation.

To identify that a figure has been reflected across a line, look for evidence that the figure is now face-down.

To identify that a figure has been translated, look for evidence that a figure is still face-up and has not changed orientation; the only change is location.

To identify that a figure has been dilated, look for evidence that the figure has changed its size but not its orientation.

Dilation

A dilation is a transformation which proportionally stretches or shrinks a figure by a scale factor. The dilated image is the same shape and orientation as the original image but a different size. A polygon and its dilated image are similar.

Using transparencies to represent transformations

After drawing a shape on a piece of transparency, the shape can be rotated by leaving the transparency on a flat surface and turning it clockwise or counterclockwise.

After drawing a shape on a piece of transparency, the shape can be translated by leaving the transparency on a flat surface and sliding it in any direction (left, right, up, down, or along a diagonal).

After drawing a shape on a piece of transparency, the shape can be reflected by turning the transparency over so that the side the shape is on the underside of the transparency, touching the table.

Using functions to represent a translation on the Cartesian plane

First, determine the points which define the shape. Second, use an equation or equations to express how the vertices of the shape are moving. When the shape is translated both vertically and horizontally, the translation can be expressed using two equations: one for the x-values and one for the y-values.

For example, consider a triangle, which is defined by its vertices at three specific ordered pairs. Adding 5 to each of the x-values will create a second triangle five units to the right of the first triangle; the equation representing this transformation is $x_2 = x_1 + 5$, where x_1 represents the x-coordinates of the original triangle and x_2 represents the x-coordinates of the translated triangle. If the triangle is also moved four units downward, the equation $y_2 = y_1 - 4$ can be used to find the new y=coordinates, represented by y_2, from the triangle's original y-coordinates, represented by y_1. Together, the horizontal and vertical shift can be written as $\begin{cases} x_2 = x_1 + 5 \\ y_2 = y_1 - 4 \end{cases}$, and these equations would be used to transform each vertex like so:

first point (x_1, y_1)	first vertex (3,6)	second vertex (5,1)	third vertex (4,−1)
x-values: $x_2 = x_1 + 5$	$x_2 = 3 + 5 = 8$	$x_2 = 5 + 5 = 10$	$x_2 = 4 + 5 = 9$
y-values: $y_2 = y_1 - 4$	$y_2 = 6 - 4 = 2$	$y_2 = 1 - 4 = -3$	$y_2 = -1 - 4 = -5$
new point (x_2, y_2)	first vertex (8,2)	second vertex (10,−3)	third vertex (9,−5)

A triangle with vertices (3,6), (5,1), and (4,-1) shifted five units to the right and four units down results in a triangle with vertices (8,2), (10,-3), and (9,-5).

Translated vs. stretched horizontally shapes

When a figure is translated, it moves to another location within the plane; since each point is shifted by the same distance, its size and shape remain the same. When a figure is stretched horizontally, its size and shape are affected. For example, consider an equilateral triangle which has a horizontal base. If the two endpoints of the base are pulled horizontally in opposite directions, the angle opposite the base widens as the two other angles become smaller. So, the lengths of the sides and the angle measures change, and the resulting triangle differs in both size and shape from the original triangle.

Rotations and reflections which carry a rectangle onto itself

A rectangle will be carried onto itself when it is rotated any multiple of 180° either clockwise or counterclockwise about its center. If the rectangle is a square, a rotation of 90° or any multiple of 90° clockwise or counterclockwise about the center will carry the square onto itself.

Any rectangle will be carried onto itself when it is rotated 360° or any multiple of 360° about any point either clockwise or counterclockwise

A rectangle will also be carried onto itself when it is reflected over any of its lines of symmetry. A rectangle has two lines of symmetry, and a square has four.

Using transformations (rotations and reflections) to carry a parallelogram onto itself.

A parallelogram will be carried onto itself when it is rotated by any multiple of 180° either clockwise or counterclockwise about its center. A square or any other rhombus is carried onto itself when it is rotated about its center by a multiple of 90°.

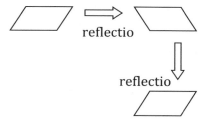

Any parallelogram will be carried onto itself when it is rotated 360° or any multiple of 360° about any point either clockwise or counterclockwise.

A square or other rhombus reflected across any of its four lines of symmetry will map onto itself, and a rectangle reflected across either of its two line of symmetry will be carried onto itself. Other parallelograms have no lines of symmetry and can therefore not be reflected onto themselves.

Rotations and reflections which carry a trapezoid onto itself

A trapezoid will be carried onto itself when it is rotated 360° or any multiple of 360° either clockwise or counterclockwise.

A trapezoid will be carried onto itself when it is reflected over its line of symmetry, which is the perpendicular bisector of its two parallel sides.

Rotations and reflections which carry a regular polygon onto itself

A regular polygon will be carried onto itself when it is rotated about its center either clockwise or counterclockwise by $360°/n$, where n is the number of sides of the polygon.

Any polygon will be carried onto itself when it is rotated 360° or any multiple of 360° about any point either clockwise or counterclockwise.

A regular polygon will be carried onto itself when it is reflected over any of its lines of symmetry.

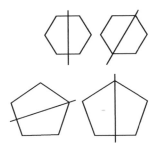

Congruence of two figures in terms of rigid motion

Two figures are congruent if one figure can be made to carry onto the second figure using one or more rotations, reflections, and/or translations.

Two triangles are congruent in terms of rigid motion when one triangle is the image of the other triangle. In one triangle, each side and angle is matched with only one side or angle of the other triangle. If a series of rigid motions align the two triangles, then the sides that are the same and the angles that are the same will be matched. If the sides and angles are all matched, then the congruent triangles have six congruent parts. Thus, the parts that correspond after transformation are congruent with each other.

Use the definition of congruence in terms of rigid motion to describe the criteria for angle-side-angle (ASA) congruence for triangles

A figure is congruent to another figure if one can be superimposed on the other by rigid motion (translation, reflection, rotation). When two congruent triangles are superimposed, it two angles and the side between the two angles align, the other two sides and angle will also align, Therefore, it is sufficient to show when proving two triangles congruent that two angles and the side between the angles are the same.

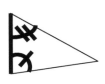 

Use the definition of congruence in terms of rigid motion to describe the criteria for side-angle-side (SAS) congruence for triangles

A figure is congruent to another figure if one can be superimposed on the other by rigid motion (translation, reflection, rotation). When two congruent triangles are superimposed, it two sides and the angle between the two angles align, the other side and two angles will also align,
Therefore, it is sufficient to show when proving two triangles congruent that two sides and the angle between the sides are the same.

Use the definition of congruence in terms of rigid motion to describe the criteria for side-side-side (SSS) congruence for triangles

A figure is congruent to another figure if one can be superimposed on the other by rigid motion (translation, reflection, rotation). When two congruent triangles are superimposed, if all three sides align, the three angles will also align, therefore, it is sufficient to show when proving two triangles congruent that the measures of the three sides of the one triangle are equal to the measures of the three sides of the other.

Show that vertical angles are congruent

Draw two lines which intersect at a point. This point of intersection becomes a shared vertex of four angles created by the intersection of the two lines. Vertical angles are across from each other, and there are two pairs of vertical angles formed by the intersection of two lines. When one angle is rotated about the point of intersection by 180°, it aligns with its vertical angle. Therefore, the two angles are congruent.

Show that when two parallel lines are cut by a transversal, the resulting alternate interior angles are congruent. Showing that when two parallel lines are cut by a transversal, the resulting corresponding angles are congruent

Draw two parallel lines cut by a transversal and note two alternate interior angles. Using the midpoint of the transversal segment between the two parallel lines as a point of rotation, rotate half of the figure onto the other half of the figure. The two noted angles align and are therefore congruent.

Draw two parallel lines cut by a transversal and note two corresponding angles. Translate one parallel line along the transversal until it aligns with the other parallel line. The two noted angles align and are therefore congruent.

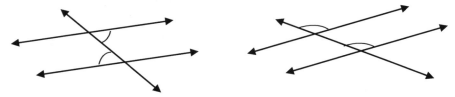

Show the measures of the interior angles of a triangle add to $180°$

Draw a line on a piece of paper. Cut each of the sides of the triangle at the midpoint to create three angles. Transform the three angles using rotation to align all three so their vertices are at the same point. Two of the angles' sides are parallel to the line, and the third angle's sides touch the other sides of the angles. Because the three angles come together to form a line, which measures $180°$, the three angles add to $180°$.

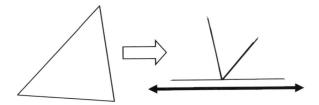

Base angles of an isosceles triangle are congruent

Draw an isosceles triangle. Reflect one side of the triangle across the perpendicular bisector of the base. The two base angles align and are therefore congruent.

Three medians of a triangle meet at a point

Draw a triangle. From each vertex, draw a line to the midpoint of the opposite side. These three medians intersect at one point in the triangle. Show that this is true for acute, right, and obtuse triangles.

Show that the segment which joins the midpoints of two sides of a triangle is parallel to the third side and half its length.

Draw a triangle and construct a line segment which connects the midpoints of two sides of the triangle. Translate the line segment so that it aligns with the third side and one endpoint of the segment is aligned with the endpoint of the third side. Since the line segment was able to be translated without rotation, it is parallel to the third side of the triangle.

Draw a line that is perpendicular to the third side of the triangle through the translated segment's endpoint which does not lie on the triangle's vertex. Reflect the line segment across this line. The endpoint that was aligned with the first vertex is now aligned with the second vertex; thus, the line segment is half the length of the third side of the triangle.

Opposite sides of parallelograms are congruent

Draw a parallelogram. Translate one side of the parallelogram along the adjacent sides until it is aligned with the opposite side. The endpoints align, so the sides are congruent.

Opposite angles of parallelograms are congruent

Use the point where the diagonals intersect as a point of rotation. Rotate the parallelogram 180° so that the angles are aligned with the angles opposite them.

Diagonals of parallelograms bisect each other

Draw a parallelogram and its two diagonals. Use one diagonal as a line of reflection. Reflect the other diagonal onto itself. Since the endpoints align, the line of reflection is a bisector of the reflected diagonal. Repeat the process for the other diagonal.

A rectangle is a parallelogram with congruent diagonals

A rectangle is a parallelogram with four right angles. Draw a rectangle and its two diagonals. Find the midpoints of two opposite sides of the rectangle and connect them to construct a line of reflection. Reflect one of the right triangles over the line of reflection. The reflected triangle's hypotenuse, which is the one of the rectangle's diagonals, aligns with another triangle's hypotenuse, which is the rectangle's other diagonal. Thus, the diagonals are congruent, so a rectangle is a parallelogram with congruent diagonals.

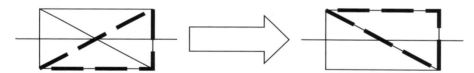

Tools used in geometric constructions

Compass – A tool used to draw circles and to measure distances from a single point. A compass is used for translations and copying figures.

Straightedge – A tool used to draw straight lines and line segments and to measure distances between two points. A straightedge is used to keep lines neat and straight when constructing or copying figures.

Protractor – A tool used to measure angles. A protractor is used for rotations and constructions of polygons.

String – A tool used to measure distances either from a single point or between two points. String is used in rotations and to copy figures.

Reflective devices – A variety of tools used to reflect an image.

Paper folding – A technique used to reflect images onto figures or portions of figures onto themselves. Paper folding is used in reflections and constructions.
Geometry software also exists to construct and copy figures on the computer.

Compass

Using a compass to construct a copy of a segment
Use a compass to measure the length of the segment by placing the stationary end on one endpoint and opening the compass so the pencil end is on the other endpoint. Draw a point elsewhere and place the compass tip on the point, then draw an arc with the pencil. Any line segment drawn from the initial point to any point on the arc will be a copy of the first segment.

Compass and a straightedge

Using a compass and a straightedge to construct a copy of an angle
Place the stationary end of a compass at the vertex of the angle and construct an arc that intersects both rays. Use a straightedge to construct a ray elsewhere, and without changing the compass opening, draw an arc by positioning the compass at its endpoint. Then, on the original angle, place the compass tip on the point where the arc intersects one of the rays and adjust the compass so that the pencil meets the point where the arc intersects the other ray; draw a small arc that passes through this point. Without changing the compass opening, place the compass tip on the intersection of the ray and the arc and draw a second arc which intersects the first. From the ray's endpoint, draw using a straightedge another ray through the intersection of the two arcs on the construction. This angle is a copy of the first angle.

Using a compass and a straightedge to construct an angle bisector
Place the compass tip on the vertex of the angle. Draw an arc that intersects both rays of the angle. Move the compass tip to one of the intersections. Draw a small arc inside the angle, beyond the first arc, making the compass opening smaller if necessary. Without changing the compass opening, move the compass tip to the other ray at the point at which it intersects the first arc. Draw another small arc inside the angle that intersects the last arc. Use a straightedge to draw a line through the vertex of the angle and the intersection of the two small arcs. This line is the angle bisector.

Using a compass and a straightedge to construct perpendicular lines
Draw two points and use a straightedge to draw a line through the points. Place the compass tip on one of the points and draw two arcs, one above the line and one below the line. Without changing the compass opening, from the other point, draw two more arcs that intersect the first two. Construct a line through these two intersections. This line is perpendicular to the first line.

Using a compass and a straightedge to construct a line segment and its perpendicular bisector
Using a straightedge, draw a line segment. Open the width of the compass so that it is greater than half the width of the line segment. Place the compass tip on one of the endpoints and draw two arcs, one above and one below the line segment. Without changing the compass opening, from the other endpoint, draw two more arcs that intersect the first

two. Using a straightedge, construct a line through these two intersections. This line is a perpendicular bisector of the line segment.

Using a compass and straightedge to construct a line parallel to a given line through a point not on the line

Start with a line and a point not on the line. Use a straightedge to draw a ray from a point on the given line through the given point. With the compass tip at the intersection of the given line and the ray, construct an arc that intersects both. Without changing the compass opening, reposition the compass tip on the given point and draw a second arc similar to the first. Then, use the first arc to set the compass with such that one part of the compass touches point where the arc crosses the ray and the point where that arc crosses the original line. Without changing the compass opening, reposition the compass again to the given point and draw an arc through the second arc. Use the straightedge to draw a line which passes through the point of intersection of the second and third arcs and the given point. This line is parallel to the given line.

Using a compass and a straightedge to inscribe an equilateral triangle inside of a circle with a given center

Draw a point on the circle. Position the tip of a compass at the center of the circle and the pencil at this point so that the width of the compass is the circle's radius. Without changing the compass width, position the compass tip at the point on the circle and use a pencil to make an arc on the circle. Move the compass tip to the point at which this arc intersects the circle and make another arc on the circle. Continue this process all the way around the circle so that its circumference is equally divided into six pieces. Connect every other point using a straight edge to inscribe an equilateral triangle inside of the circle.

Using a compass and a straightedge to inscribe a square inside of a circle with a given center

Draw a diameter of the circle. Open the width of a compass so that it is greater than half the circle's radius. Place the compass tip at one of the endpoints of the diameter and draw an arc. Reposition the tip at the other endpoint and draw a second arc which intersects the first. Position a straightedge through this point of intersection and the center of the circle and draw a second diameter, which is the perpendicular bisector of the first. The endpoints of each of the two diameters are the vertices of a square. Connect the four vertices with a straight line to create a square inscribed in a circle.

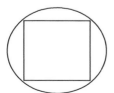

Using a compass and a straight edge to inscribe a regular hexagon inside of a circle with a given center

Draw a point on the circle. Position the tip of a compass at the center of the circle and the pencil at this point so that the width of the compass is the circle's radius. Without changing the compass width, position the compass tip at the point on the circle and use a pencil to make an arc on the circle. Move the compass tip to the point at which this arc intersects the circle and make another arc on the circle. Continue this process all the way around the circle so that its circumference is equally divided into six pieces. Connect each of these points using a straight edge to construct a regular hexagon inside of the circle.

Paper folding

Using paper folding to construct a segment bisector

Fold the paper so that the endpoints of the line segment align. The point where the fold intersects the line segment is the midpoint. Any line, line segment, or ray drawn through this point is a segment bisector.

Using paper folding to construct a line parallel to a given line through a point not on the line

Start with a line and a point not on that line, both drawn on a sheet of paper. Fold the paper so that the fold passes through the point and so that the line is reflected onto itself over the fold. Unfold the paper and fold again, again so that the fold passes through the point not on the line, but so that the first fold is reflected onto itself. Unfold the paper and use a straightedge to draw a line along the second fold. This line is parallel to the first line and passes through the point not on the line.

Similarity, Right Triangles, and Trigonometry

Verifying that a dilation takes a line not passing through the center of the dilation to a parallel line, and leaves a line passing through the center unchanged

$\overleftrightarrow{AB}$ is a line that does not pass through the center of the dilation. When line segment $\overline{AB}$ is dilated using a scale factor of 2, line segment $\overline{A'B'}$ is created. Translate the intersection of $\overleftrightarrow{AB}$ and the line through A and the center of dilation to the intersection of $\overleftrightarrow{A'B'}$ and the line through A and the center of dilation. Since $\overleftrightarrow{AB}$ overlaps $\overleftrightarrow{A'B'}$, the two lines are parallel.

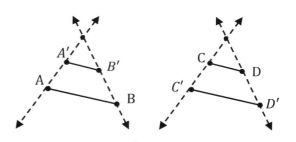

$\overleftrightarrow{CD}$ is a line that passes through the center of the dilation. When line segment $\overline{CD}$ is dilated using a scale factor of 2, $\overline{C'D'}$ is created. Both lines $\overleftrightarrow{CD}$ and $\overleftrightarrow{C'D'}$ are the same line which passes through the center of dilation, so the dilation left the line unchanged.

Verifying that a dilation of a line segment is longer or shorter than the original line segment in the ratio given by the scale factor

$\overline{AB}$ is a line segment that is dilated using a scale factor of ½. Translate $\overline{AB}$ along one line through the center of dilation until A is aligned with A'. Since the ratio is less than 1, $\overline{AB}$ is larger than $\overline{A'B'}$, so using the perpendicular bisector of $\overline{AB}$ as a line of reflection, reflect $\overline{A'B'}$ so that A' is now aligned with B. Since B' did not move, and is still at the point of intersection between $\overline{AB}$ and the perpendicular bisector, the ratio of $\overline{A'B'}$ to $\overline{AB}$ is 1 to 2.

$\overline{CD}$ is a line segment that is dilated using a scale factor of 2. Translate $\overline{CD}$ along one line through the center of dilation until C is aligned with C'. Since the ratio is greater than 1, $\overline{C'D'}$ is larger than $\overline{CD}$, so using the perpendicular bisector of $\overline{C'D'}$ as a line of reflection, reflect $\overline{CD}$ so that C is now aligned with D'. Since D did not move, and is still at the point of intersection between $\overline{C'D'}$ and the perpendicular bisector, the ratio of $\overline{C'D'}$ to $\overline{CD}$ is 2 to 1.

Using transformations and the definition of similarity to prove that two figures are similar

The corresponding angles of similar figures are congruent, and the corresponding sides are proportional. Rotate and translate one figure onto the other so that one pair of corresponding angles aligns. Continue to translate the figure so that corresponding angles are aligned, one pair of angles at a time. After verifying that all pairs of corresponding angles are congruent, determine if the sides are proportional. Position the figures so that corresponding sides are parallel and so that the smaller figure does not overlap the larger figure. Use a straightedge to draw lines that will connect each pair of corresponding

- 15 -

vertices. Extend the lines to find a point of possible intersection. If all the lines meet at a single point, that point is the center of dilation and the two figures are similar.

Using transformations and the definition of similarity to show two triangles are similar if all corresponding pairs of angles are congruent and all corresponding pairs of sides are proportional

Rotate and translate one triangle so that one pair of corresponding angles aligns. Continue to translate the triangle so that corresponding angles are aligned, one pair of angles at a time. After verifying that all pairs of corresponding angles are congruent, determine if the sides are proportional. Position the triangles so that corresponding sides are parallel and so that the smaller triangle does not overlap the larger. Use a straightedge to draw lines that will connect each pair of corresponding vertices. Extend the lines to find a point of possible intersection. If all the lines meet at a single point, that point is the center of dilation and the two figures are similar.

Using the properties of similarity transformations to describe the criteria for angle-angle (AA) similarity of triangles

When a triangle is dilated (a similarity transformation) the lengths of its side change, but its angle measures remain the same. When an angle of a triangle is aligned with the corresponding angle of a dilated triangle, the two angles match; the same is true for the other two pairs of corresponding angles. When the corresponding angles of two triangles are congruent, the two triangles are similar. It is sufficient, however, to show that two of the three pairs of corresponding angles are congruent to determine the triangles' similarity: the third pair of corresponding angles must also be congruent since the sum of the angles in each triangle is 180°.

Proving that a line which passes through a triangle and which is parallel to one of its sides divides the other two sides proportionally

In the diagram, PQ is parallel to BC. When two parallel lines are cut by a transversal, corresponding angles are congruent. So, $\angle APQ \cong \angle PBC$ and, $\angle AQP \cong \angle QCB$. Thus, by the AA similarity theorem, $\triangle ABC$ is similar to $\triangle APQ$. The ratios of corresponding sides of similar triangles are proportional, so $\frac{AB}{AP} = \frac{AC}{AQ}$. Since $AB = AP + PB$ and $AC = AQ + QC$,

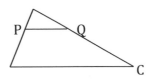

$\frac{AP+PB}{AP} = \frac{AQ+QC}{AQ}$. This can be rewritten as $\frac{AP}{AP} + \frac{PB}{AP} = \frac{AQ}{AQ} + \frac{QC}{AQ} \rightarrow 1 + \frac{PB}{AP} = 1 + \frac{QC}{AQ} \rightarrow \frac{PB}{AP} = \frac{QC}{AQ}$. Therefore, a line which passes through a triangle and which is parallel to one of its sides divides the other two sides proportionally.

Proving a line that divides two sides of a triangle proportionally is parallel to the third side

If line PQ divides $\triangle ABC$ proportionally, then $\frac{PB}{AP} = \frac{QC}{AQ}$.

$$\frac{PB}{AP} = \frac{QC}{AQ}$$
$$1 + \frac{PB}{AP} = 1 + \frac{QC}{AQ}$$
$$\frac{AP}{AP} + \frac{PB}{AP} = \frac{AQ}{AQ} + \frac{QC}{AQ}$$
$$\frac{AP + PB}{AP} = \frac{AQ + QC}{AQ}$$

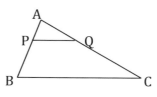

Since $AB = AP + PB$ and $AC = AQ + QC$, $\frac{AB}{AP} = \frac{AC}{AQ}$. Since $\angle BAC$ is shared with $\triangle ABC$ and $\triangle APQ$, and since the two sides flanking the angle are proportional, by SAS similarity, $\triangle ABC$ is similar to $\triangle APQ$. Corresponding angles of similar triangles are congruent, so $\angle APQ \cong \angle PBC$ and , $\angle AQP \cong \angle QCB$. When two lines, such as PQ and BC, are cut by a transversal, such as AB, and corresponding angles, such as so $\angle APQ$ and $\angle PBC$ are congruent, the two lines are parallel. So, PQ is parallel to BC. Therefore, a line that divides two sides of a triangle proportionally is parallel to the third side.

Proving the Pythagorean Theorem using similar triangles

To prove the Pythagorean Theorem for right $\triangle ABC$, show $(AB)^2 + (BC)^2 = (AC)^2$. Identify three similar triangles created by drawing altitude $\overline{BD}$. Use rotation and translation to verify that the three triangles are similar by AA. $\triangle ABC \sim \triangle BDC \sim \triangle ADB$. Similar triangles have proportional sides, so $\frac{AB}{AD} = \frac{AC}{AB}$ and $\frac{BC}{DC} = \frac{AC}{BC}$. Also note, $AD + DC = AC$.

Use cross multiplication:	$\frac{AB}{AD} = \frac{AC}{AB} \rightarrow (AB)^2 = (AD)(AC)$ $\frac{BC}{DC} = \frac{AC}{BC} \rightarrow (BC)^2 = (DC)(AC)$
Add these two new equations together:	$(AB)^2 + (BC)^2 = (AD)(AC) + (DC)(AC).$
Use the distributive property to simplify the right side:	$(AB)^2 + (BC)^2 = (AD + DC)(AC)$
Use substitution:	$(AB)^2 + (BC)^2 = (AC)(AC)$
Simplify:	$(AB)^2 + (BC)^2 = (AC)^2$

(drawings not to scale)

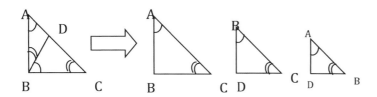

Using triangle congruence (ASA) to solve problems and prove relationships in geometric figures

Triangle congruence (ASA) can be used to solve problems involving triangles when two pairs of corresponding angles are known to be congruent and the contained sides are also congruent. To solve for the third angle, subtract the sum of the known angles from 180°. Once triangle congruence is established, all other corresponding parts of the triangles can also be identified as congruent.

Given $\triangle ABC$ and $\triangle DEF$.

1. Show $\triangle ABC \cong \triangle DEF$.

2. Find the length of AC.

3. Find the measure of $\angle F$.

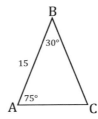
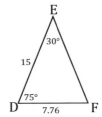

1. Since $m\angle A = m\angle D = 75°$, $AB = DE = 15$, and $m\angle B = m\angle E = 30°$, $\triangle ABC \cong \triangle DEF$ by Angle-Side-Angle Congruence.

2. Since corresponding parts of congruent triangles are congruent, $AC = DF = 7.76$.

3. Since the sum of the angles in a triangle is 180°, add the measure of $\angle D$ and the measure of $\angle E$ and subtract from 180°: $180° - (75° + 30°) = 180° - 105° = 75°$. $m\angle F = 75°$.

Using triangle congruence (SAS) to solve problems and prove relationships in geometric figures

Triangle congruence (SAS) can be used to solve problems involving triangles when two pairs of corresponding sides are known to be congruent and the contained angles are also congruent. Once triangle congruence is established, all other corresponding parts of the triangles can also be identified as congruent.

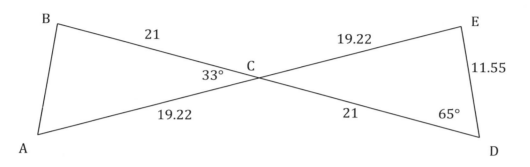

Given $\triangle ABC$ and $\triangle EDC$.

1. Show $\triangle ABC \cong \triangle EDC$.

2. Find the length of AB.

3. Find the measure of $\angle E$.

1. Since $BC = DC = 21$, $\angle BCA \cong \angle DCE$ (vertical angles), and $AC = EC = 19.22$, $\triangle ABC \cong \triangle DEF$ by Side-Angle-Side Congruence.

2. Since Corresponding Parts of Congruent Triangles are Congruent, $AB = ED = 11.55$.

3. The sum of the angles in a triangle is 180°.

$$\angle C + \angle D + \angle E = 180°$$
$$33° + 65° + \angle E = 180°$$
$$98° + \angle E = 180°$$
$$\angle E = 82°$$

Using triangle congruence (SSS) to solve problems and prove relationships in geometric figures

Triangle congruence (SSS) can be used to solve problems involving triangles when all pairs of corresponding sides are known to be congruent. Once triangle congruence is established, all other corresponding parts of the triangles can also be identified as congruent.

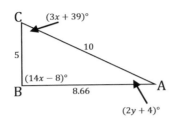 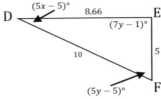

Given $\triangle ABC$ and $\triangle DEF$,

1. Show $\triangle ABC \cong \triangle DEF$.

2. Find the measure of $\angle D$.

3. Find the measure of $\angle E$.

4. Find the measure of $\angle F$.

1. Since $AB = DE = 8.66$, $BC = EF = 5$, and $AC = DF = 10$, $\triangle ABC \cong \triangle DEF$ by Side-Side-Side Congruence.

2. Since the sum of the angles in a triangle add to 180°, write an equation for each triangle.

$\triangle ABC$:	$\triangle EDC$:
$(2y + 4) + (14x - 8) + (3x + 39)$ $= 180$ $17x + 2y + 35 = 180$ $17x + 2y = 145$ $y = \frac{145 - 17x}{2}$	$(5x - 5) + (5y - 5) + (7y - 1) = 180$ $5x + 12y - 11 = 180$ $5x + 12y = 191$

Solve the system of equations.

| $5x + 12\left(\frac{145 - 17x}{2}\right) = 191$ $5x + 870 - 102x = 191$ $-97x = -679$ $x = 7$ | $y = \frac{145 - 17(7)}{2}$ $y = \frac{145 - 119}{2} = \frac{26}{2}$ $y = 13$ |

$m\angle D = 5x - 5 = 5(7) - 5 = 35 - 5 = 30°$.

3. $m\angle E = 7y - 1 = 7(13) - 1 = 91 - 1 = 90°$.

4. $m\angle F = 5y - 5 = 5(13) - 5 = 65 - 5 = 60°$.

Using triangle similarity (AA) to solve problems and prove relationships in geometric figures

Triangle similarity (AA) can be used to solve problems involving triangles when two pairs of corresponding angles are known to be congruent. To solve for the third angle, subtract the sum of the known angles from 180°. Once triangle similarity is established, all pairs of corresponding angles in the triangles can be identified as congruent and all pairs of corresponding sides in the triangles can be identified as proportional.

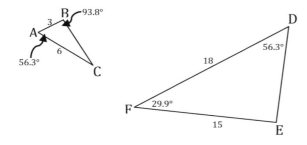

Given $\triangle ABC$ and $\triangle DEF$

1. Find the measure of $\angle E$.

2. Find the measure of $\angle C$.

3. Show $\triangle ABC \sim \triangle DEF$.

4. Find the length of DE.

5. Find the length of BC.

1. Since the sum of the angles of a triangle is 180°, $m\angle E = 180° - (29.9° + 56.3°) = 180° - 86.2° = 93.8°$.

2. Since the sum of the angles of a triangle is 180°, $m\angle C = 180° - (56.3° + 93.8°) = 180° - 150.1° = 29.9°$.

3. Since $m\angle A = m\angle D = 56.3°$ and $m\angle B = m\angle E = 93.8°$, $\triangle ABC \sim \triangle DEF$ by Angle-Angle Similarity.

4. Since corresponding sides are proportional in similar triangles, $\frac{AB}{DE} = \frac{AC}{DF}. \frac{3}{DE} = \frac{6}{18} \rightarrow 54 = 6 \cdot DE \rightarrow DE = 9$.

5. Since corresponding sides are proportional in similar triangles, $\frac{BC}{EF} = \frac{AC}{DF}. \frac{BC}{15} = \frac{6}{18} \rightarrow 18 \cdot BC = 90 \rightarrow BC = 5$.

Trigonometric ratio sine for an acute angle using ratios of sides in similar right triangles

Similar triangles have three pairs of congruent angles and three pairs of proportional sides. The proportion has the same value for all pairs of sides, so $\frac{a}{d} = \frac{c}{f}$ or (using cross multiplication and division to reorganize) $\frac{a}{c} = \frac{d}{f}$. The trigonometric ratio sine is opposite over hypotenuse. In $\triangle ABC$, $\sin A = \frac{a}{c}$ and in $\triangle DEF$, $\sin D = \frac{d}{f}$. So since $\frac{a}{c} = \frac{d}{f}$, $\sin A = \sin D$. This shows that the trigonometric ratio sine is a property of the angle because the ratio is the same in both triangles even though the triangles are different sizes.

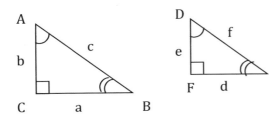

Trigonometric ratio cosine for an acute angle using ratios of sides in similar right triangles

Similar triangles have three pairs of congruent angles and three pairs of proportional sides. The proportion has the same value for all pairs of sides, so $\frac{b}{e} = \frac{c}{f}$ or (using cross multiplication and division to reorganize) $\frac{b}{c} = \frac{e}{f}$. The trigonometric ratio cosine is adjacent over hypotenuse. In $\triangle ABC$, $\cos A = \frac{b}{c}$ and in $\triangle DEF$, $\cos D = \frac{e}{f}$. So since $\frac{b}{c} = \frac{e}{f}$, $\cos A = \cos D$. This shows that the trigonometric ratio cosine is a property of the angle because the ratio is the same in both triangles even though the triangles are different sizes.

Trigonometric ratio tangent for an acute angle using ratios of sides in similar right triangles

Similar triangles have three pairs of congruent angles and three pairs of proportional sides. The proportion has the same value for all pairs of sides, so $\frac{a}{d} = \frac{b}{e}$ or (using cross multiplication and division to reorganize) $\frac{a}{b} = \frac{d}{e}$. The trigonometric ratio tangent is opposite over adjacent. In $\triangle ABC$, $\tan A = \frac{a}{b}$ and in $\triangle DEF$, $\tan D = \frac{d}{e}$. So since $\frac{a}{b} = \frac{d}{e}$, $\tan A = \tan D$. This shows that the trigonometric ratio tangent is a property of the angle because the ratio is the same in both triangles even though the triangles are different sizes.

Relationship between sine and cosine of complementary angles

The sum of two complementary angles is 90°. In a right triangle, the two acute angles are complementary because the sum of the angles (180°) minus the right angle (90°) leaves the sum of the acute angles (90°). So, $m\angle A + m\angle B = 90°$. $\sin A = \frac{opp}{hyp} = \frac{a}{c}$ and $\cos B = \frac{adj}{hyp} = \frac{a}{c}$, thus the sine of an angle is equal to the cosine of its complementary angle.

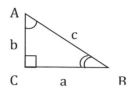

Using sine to solve problems involving right triangles

Problems that can be solved using sine must give specific information and ask for a specific solution.

Given	Unknown
one acute angle and the side opposite that angle	the hypotenuse
one acute angle and the hypotenuse	the side opposite that angle
the hypotenuse and one leg	the angle opposite the known leg **to solve this problem, use $\sin^{-1}$**

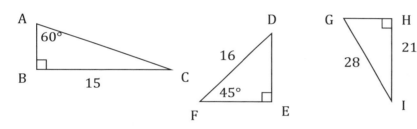

Given $\triangle ABC$, $\triangle DEF$, and $\triangle GHI$,

1. Solve for the length of the hypotenuse in $\triangle ABC$.

2. Solve for the length of DE in $\triangle DEF$.

3. Solve for the measure of $\angle G$ in $\triangle GHI$.

1. In $\triangle ABC$, AC is the hypotenuse and $\sin A = \frac{BC}{AC}$. So, $\sin 60 = \frac{15}{AC} \rightarrow AC = \frac{15}{\sin 60} = 17.32$.

2. In $\triangle DEF$, $\sin F = \frac{DE}{DF}$. So, $\sin 45 = \frac{DE}{16} \rightarrow DE = 16 \cdot \sin 45 = 11.31$.

3. In $\triangle GHI$, $\sin G = \frac{HI}{GI}$. So, $\sin G = \frac{21}{28} \rightarrow G = \sin^{-1}\frac{21}{28} = 48.59°$.

- 23 -

Using cosine to solve problems involving right triangles

Problems that can be solved using cosine must give specific information and ask for a specific solution.

Given	Unknown
one acute angle and the side adjacent to that angle	the hypotenuse
one acute angle and the hypotenuse	the side adjacent to that angle
the hypotenuse and one side	the angle adjacent to the known side **to solve this problem, use $\cos^{-1}$**

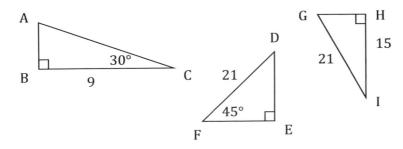

Given $\triangle ABC$, $\triangle DEF$, and $\triangle GHI$,

1. Solve for the length of the hypotenuse in $\triangle ABC$.

2. Solve for the length of EF in $\triangle DEF$.

3. Solve for the measure of $\angle I$ in $\triangle GHI$.

1. In $\triangle ABC$, AC is the hypotenuse and $\cos C = \frac{BC}{AC}$. So, $\cos 30 = \frac{9}{AC} \rightarrow AC = \frac{9}{\cos 30} = 10.39$.

2. In $\triangle DEF$, $\cos F = \frac{EF}{DF}$. So, $\cos 45 = \frac{EF}{21} \rightarrow EF = 21 \cdot \cos 45 = 14.85$.

3. In $\triangle GHI$, $\cos I = \frac{HI}{GI}$. So, $\cos I = \frac{15}{21} \rightarrow I = \cos^{-1}\frac{15}{21} = 44.42°$.

Using tangent to solve problems involving right triangles

Problems that can be solved using tangent must give specific information and ask for a specific solution.

Given	Unknown
one acute angle and the side opposite that angle	the side adjacent to that angle
one acute angle and the side adjacent to that angle	the side opposite that angle
two legs	either of the two acute angles **to solve this problem, use $\tan^{-1}$**

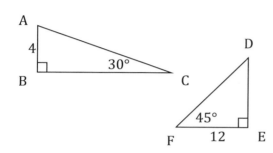
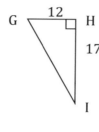

Given $\triangle ABC$, $\triangle DEF$, and $\triangle GHI$,

1. Solve for the length of BC in $\triangle ABC$.

2. Solve for the length of DE in $\triangle DEF$.

3. Solve for the measure of $\angle I$ in $\triangle GHI$.

1. In $\triangle ABC$, $\tan C = \frac{AB}{BC}$. So, $\tan 30 = \frac{4}{BC} \rightarrow BC = \frac{4}{\tan 30} = 6.93$.

2. In $\triangle DEF$, $\tan F = \frac{DE}{EF}$. So, $\tan 45 = \frac{DE}{12} \rightarrow DE = 12 \cdot \tan 45 = 12$.

3. In $\triangle GHI$, $\tan I = \frac{GH}{HI}$. So, $\tan I = \frac{12}{17} \rightarrow I = \tan^{-1}\frac{12}{17} = 35.22°$.

Using the Pythagorean Theorem to solve problems involving right triangles

Problems that can be solved using the Pythagorean Theorem must give specific information and ask for a specific solution.

Given	Unknown
two legs	the hypotenuse
one leg and the hypotenuse	the other leg

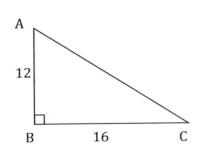
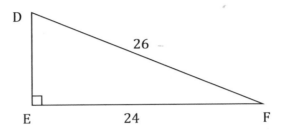

Given $\triangle ABC$ and $\triangle DEF$,

1. Solve for the length of AC in $\triangle ABC$.

2. Solve for the length of DE in $\triangle DEF$.

1. In $\triangle ABC$, $AB^2 + BC^2 = AC^2$. So, $12^2 + 16^2 = AC^2 \rightarrow AC^2 = 144 + 256 = 400 \rightarrow AC = \sqrt{400} = 20$.

2. In $\triangle DEF$, $DE^2 + EF^2 = DF^2$. So, $DE^2 + 24^2 = 26^2 \rightarrow DE^2 + 576 = 676 \rightarrow DE^2 = 676 - 576 = 100 \rightarrow DE = \sqrt{100} = 10$

From the triangle area formula $Area = \frac{1}{2}bh$, where b is the length of triangle's base, and h is the triangle's height, derive the formula $Area_{\triangle ABC} = \frac{1}{2} \cdot a \cdot b \cdot \sin C$ by drawing an auxiliary line from a vertex perpendicular to the opposite side.

$Area_{\triangle ABC} = \frac{1}{2} \cdot b \cdot h$. Notice that h is an auxiliary line from the vertex, B, and perpendicular to the opposite side, AC, and h divides $\triangle ABC$ into two right triangles. From the triangle on the right, $\sin C = \frac{h}{a}$, so $h = a \cdot \sin C$. Substituting this into the area formula creates $Area_{\triangle ABC} = \frac{1}{2} \cdot b \cdot (a \cdot \sin C)$, which can be written $Area_{\triangle ABC} = \frac{1}{2} \cdot a \cdot b \cdot \sin C$.

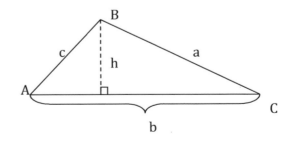

Prove the Law of Sines

The Law of Sines states that for any $\triangle ABC$, $\frac{\sin A}{a} = \frac{\sin B}{b} = \frac{\sin C}{c}$. To prove this, draw an auxiliary line from the vertex at B, perpendicular to AC. Notice that $\sin A = \frac{h}{c}$, so $\frac{\sin A}{a} = \frac{\frac{h}{c}}{a} = \frac{h}{c} \cdot \frac{1}{a} = \frac{h}{a \cdot c}$. Notice that $\sin C = \frac{h}{a}$, so $\frac{\sin C}{c} = \frac{\frac{h}{a}}{c} = \frac{h}{a} \cdot \frac{1}{c} = \frac{h}{a \cdot c}$. Therefore, $\frac{\sin A}{a} = \frac{\sin C}{c}$.

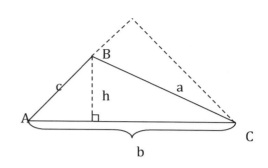

Now, draw an auxiliary line (call it g) from another vertex C) perpendicular to the opposite side AB to create two other right triangles. Notice that $\sin A = \frac{g}{b}$, so $\frac{\sin A}{a} = \frac{\frac{g}{b}}{a} = \frac{g}{b} \cdot \frac{1}{a} = \frac{g}{a \cdot b}$. Notice that $\sin B = \frac{g}{a}$, so $\frac{\sin B}{b} = \frac{\frac{g}{a}}{b} = \frac{g}{a} \cdot \frac{1}{b} = \frac{g}{a \cdot b}$. Therefore, $\frac{\sin A}{a} = \frac{\sin B}{b}$. Since $\frac{\sin A}{a} = \frac{\sin C}{c}$ and $\frac{\sin A}{a} = \frac{\sin B}{b}$ are both true, $\frac{\sin A}{a} = \frac{\sin B}{b} = \frac{\sin C}{c}$ is also true.

Prove the Law of Cosines

The Law of Cosines states: $c^2 = a^2 + b^2 - 2 \cdot a \cdot b \cdot \cos C$. To prove this, draw an auxiliary line from the vertex at B, perpendicular to AC. Side b is now split into two lengths, x and $b - x$.

use the Pythagorean Theorem to write an equation about the right triangle with hypotenuse a	$a^2 = x^2 + h^2$
use trigonometry to write a cosine equation about angle C	$\cos C = \dfrac{x}{a}$ $x = a \cdot \cos C$
use the Pythagorean Theorem two write an equation about the right triangle with hypotenuse c	$c^2 = (b - x)^2 + h^2$ $c^2 = (b^2 - 2 \cdot b \cdot x + x^2) + h^2$ $c^2 = b^2 - 2 \cdot b \cdot x + (x^2 + h^2)$
substitute a^2 for $(x^2 + h^2)$	$c^2 = b^2 - 2 \cdot b \cdot x + a^2$ $c^2 = a^2 + b^2 - 2 \cdot b \cdot x$
substitute $a \cdot \cos C$ for x	$c^2 = a^2 + b^2 - 2 \cdot b \cdot (a \cdot \cos C)$ $c^2 = a^2 + b^2 - 2 \cdot a \cdot b \cdot \cos C$

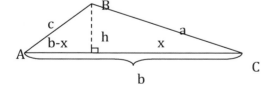

Using the Law of Sines to solve problems involving triangles

Problems that can be solved using the Law of Sines must give specific information and ask for a specific solution.

Given	Unknown
two sides and an angle opposite one side	the angle opposite the other side
two angles and a side (find the third angle using the Angle Sum Theorem if necessary)	the side opposite any angle

Given $\triangle ABC$ and $\triangle DEF$,

1. Find the measure of $\angle C$.

2. Find the measure of $\angle A$.

3. Find the length of BC.

4. Find the measure of $\angle E$.

5. Find the length of DE.

6. Find the length of DF.

1. $\frac{\sin C}{AB} = \frac{\sin B}{AC} \rightarrow \frac{\sin C}{7.5} = \frac{\sin 63}{10} \rightarrow \sin C = \frac{7.5 \cdot \sin 63}{10} = 0.668 \rightarrow C = \sin^{-1} 0.668 = 41.9°.$

2. Since the sum of the angles in a triangle is 180°, $m\angle A = 180 - (63 + 41.9) = 180 - 104.9 = 75.1°.$

3. $\frac{\sin A}{BC} = \frac{\sin B}{AC} \rightarrow \frac{\sin 75.1}{BC} = \frac{\sin 63}{10} \rightarrow BC \cdot \sin 63 = 10 \cdot \sin 75.1 \rightarrow BC = \frac{10 \cdot \sin 75.1}{\sin 63} = 10.85.$

4. Since the sum of the angles in a triangle is 180°, $m\angle E = 180 - (72 + 74) = 180 - 146 = 34°.$

5. $\frac{\sin F}{DE} = \frac{\sin D}{EF} \rightarrow \frac{\sin 74}{DE} = \frac{\sin 72}{15} \rightarrow DE \cdot \sin 72 = 15 \cdot \sin 74 \rightarrow DE = \frac{15 \cdot \sin 74}{\sin 72} = 15.16.$

6. $\frac{\sin E}{DF} = \frac{\sin D}{EF} \rightarrow \frac{\sin 34}{DF} = \frac{\sin 72}{15} \rightarrow DF \cdot \sin 72 = 15 \cdot \sin 34 \rightarrow DF = \frac{15 \cdot \sin 34}{\sin 72} = 8.82.$

Using the Law of Cosines to solve problems involving triangles.

Problems that can be solved using the Law of Cosines must give specific information and ask for a specific solution.

Given	Unknown	Form of the Equation
two sides and the angle between them	the third side	$c^2 = a^2 + b^2 - 2 \cdot a \cdot b \cdot \cos C$
three sides	any angle	$\cos C = \dfrac{a^2 + b^2 - c^2}{2 \cdot a \cdot b}$

Given $\triangle ABC$ and $\triangle DEF$, use the Law of Cosines to

1. Find the length of BC.

2. Find the measure of $\angle B$.

3. Find the measure of $\angle C$.

4. Find the measure of $\angle D$.

5. Find the measure of $\angle E$.

6. Find the measure of $\angle F$.

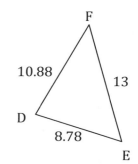

1. $BC^2 = AB^2 + AC^2 - 2 \cdot AB \cdot AC \cdot \cos A = (29.41)^2 + (17.5)^2 - 2 \cdot (29.41) \cdot (17.5) \cdot \cos 36 = 338.436 \rightarrow BC = \sqrt{338.436} = 18.40$

2. $\cos B = \dfrac{AB^2 + BC^2 - AC^2}{2 \cdot AB \cdot BC} = \dfrac{29.41^2 + 18.4^2 - 17.5^2}{2 \cdot 29.41 \cdot 18.4} = 0.829 \rightarrow B = \cos^{-1} 0.829 = 34°.$

3. $\cos C = \dfrac{BC^2 + AC^2 - AB^2}{2 \cdot BC \cdot AC} = \dfrac{18.4^2 + 17.5^2 - 29.41^2}{2 \cdot 18.4 \cdot 17.5} = -0.342 \rightarrow C = \cos^{-1} -0.342 = 110°.$

4. $\cos D = \dfrac{DE^2 + DF^2 - EF^2}{2 \cdot DE \cdot DF} = \dfrac{8.78^2 + 10.88^2 - 13^2}{2 \cdot 8.78 \cdot 10.88} = 0.139 \rightarrow D = \cos^{-1} 0.139 = 82.04°.$

5. $\cos E = \dfrac{DE^2 + EF^2 - DF^2}{2 \cdot DE \cdot EF} = \dfrac{8.78^2 + 13^2 - 10.88^2}{2 \cdot 8.78 \cdot 13} = 0.559 \rightarrow E = \cos^{-1} 0.559 = 55.98°.$

6. $\cos F = \dfrac{DF^2 + EF^2 - DE^2}{2 \cdot DF \cdot EF} = \dfrac{10.88^2 + 13^2 - 8.78^2}{2 \cdot 10.88 \cdot 13} = 0.743 \rightarrow F = \cos^{-1} 0.743 = 41.98°.$

Use the Law of Sines and the illustration to solve the following problem:

Bob is camping near a river. Bob walks upstream and finds a place to cross the river (point A). Then he turns and walks along stream for 40 feet until he is past the camp and at another river crossing (point B). How far is Bob from the tent at each crossing?

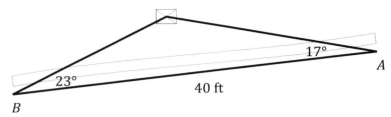

The Law of Sines is used to solve for an unknown side when two angles and one of the sides opposite an angle are known. In this problem, it is possible to find the third angle, which is opposite the known side, and use it to solve for the two missing side lengths.

$$m\angle tent = 180 - (23 + 17) = 180 - 40 = 140°.$$

$\frac{\sin tent}{AB} = \frac{\sin B}{b} \rightarrow \frac{\sin 140}{40} = \frac{\sin 23}{b} \rightarrow b \cdot \sin 140 = 40 \cdot \sin 23 \rightarrow b = \frac{40 \cdot \sin 23}{\sin 140} = 23.31.$ The distance from the tent to the first crossing is 23.31 feet.

$\frac{\sin tent}{AB} = \frac{\sin A}{a} \rightarrow \frac{\sin 140}{40} = \frac{\sin 17}{a} \rightarrow a \cdot \sin 140 = 40 \cdot \sin 17 \rightarrow a = \frac{40 \cdot \sin 17}{\sin 140} = 18.19.$ The distance from the second crossing to the tent is 18.19 feet.

Use the Law of Sines to solve the following problem:

Seth is building a tree house in a 15-foot tree on a hill in his backyard. At the base of the tree are rosebushes, which his mother will not let him remove. Seth has decided to build a 23.7-foot ladder from the base of the hill to the top of the tree. If the tree meets the ground at a 115° angle, at what angle will the ladder meet the hill?

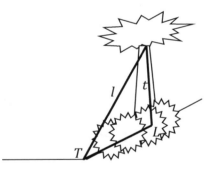

The Law of Sines is used to solve for an angle when another angle and the two sides opposite those angles are known.

$$\frac{\sin L}{l} = \frac{\sin T}{t} \rightarrow \frac{\sin 115}{23.7} = \frac{\sin T}{15} \rightarrow 23.7 \cdot \sin T = 15 \cdot \sin 115 \rightarrow \sin T = \frac{15 \cdot \sin 115}{23.7}$$
$$= 0.574 \rightarrow T = \sin^{-1} 0.574 = 35°$$

The ladder will meet the hill at an angle of 35°.

Use the Law of Cosines to solve the following problem:

Sally is flying her plane on the heading shown in the figure. The plane's instrument panel indicates an air speed of 140 mph. However, there is a crosswind of 53 mph. What is the apparent speed (x) of the plane to an observer on the ground?

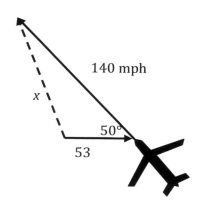

The Law of Cosines is used to solve for the third side in a triangle when two sides and the angle between them are known.

$$x^2 = (53)^2 + (140)^2 - 2 \cdot 53 \cdot 140 \cdot \cos 50 = 12870.03 \rightarrow x = \sqrt{12870.03} = 113.45 \text{ mph.}$$

Use the Law of Cosines to solve the following problem:

Beth is returning to her campsite from an ATV ride when she remembers she still has to pay for the campsite. Earlier, she entered the locations of her campsite and the ranger station into her GPS. The GPS tells her that she is 5 miles from her tent and 8 miles from the ranger station. If Beth also knows that her tent is 4 miles from the ranger station, how many degrees must she alter her course to pay the bill before returning to her campsite?

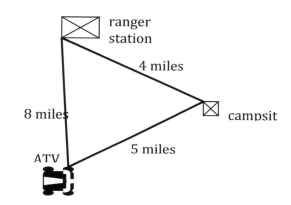

The Law of Cosines is used to solve for an angle in a triangle when three sides are known.

$$\cos A = \frac{AR^2 + AC^2 - CR^2}{2 \cdot AR \cdot AC} = \frac{8^2 + 5^2 - 4^2}{2 \cdot 8 \cdot 5} = 0.9125 \rightarrow A = \cos^{-1} 0.9125 = 24.15°.$$

Beth must alter her course by 24.15° toward the ranger station to reach the ranger station.

Circles

Proving that all circles are similar

Similar figures have the same shape but not necessarily the same size. Similar polygons have congruent corresponding angles and proportional sides. To extend this idea to circles, consider an arbitrary number of points along the circle. If points are chosen in such a way that the angles created by the radii to those points are congruent when measured from a horizontal radius, then the corresponding angles are congruent. If the ratios of corresponding radii are found and compared, the results would be proportional, thus all circles are similar.

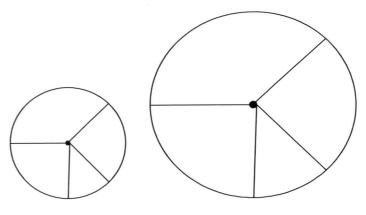

Relationship between (1) central angles and inscribed angles and (2) central angles and circumscribed angles

All of these angles have rays which pass through the same points on the circle at B and C. A central angle's vertex is at the same point as the center of a circle. An inscribed angle's vertex is on a point on the circle. A circumscribed angle's vertex is outside the circle, and its rays are tangent to the circle.

$$m\angle BDC = \frac{1}{2} \cdot m\angle BAC$$

$$m\angle BEC = 180 - m\angle BAC$$

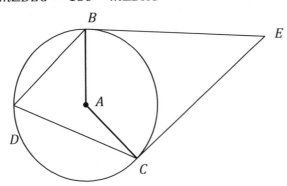

Relationship between inscribed angles whose endpoints lie on a diameter. Relationship between a tangent and the radius at the point of tangency

The measure of all inscribed angles is equal to half the intercepted arc. Since a diameter creates an arc of 180°, all inscribed angles whose endpoints lie on a diameter have a measure of 90°, are right angles, and are congruent.

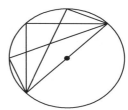

A tangent intersects a circle at only one point. The radius is a line segment from the center of the circle to a point on a circle. A tangent is perpendicular to the radius at the point of tangency.

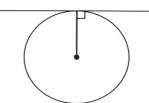

Construction of a circle inscribed in a triangle

Given a triangle, construct the angle bisectors of each of its angles. Place the compass tip on one of the vertices, open the compass and draw an arc that intersects both rays of the angle. Open the compass a little further and move the stationary end to one of the side-arc intersections. Make a small arc beyond the first arc. Without changing the compass opening, move the stationary end to the other side-arc intersection. Make another small arc that intersects the last small arc. Use a straightedge to draw a line through the angle vertex and the point of intersection for the two small arcs. Repeat these steps for the other two vertices of the triangle.

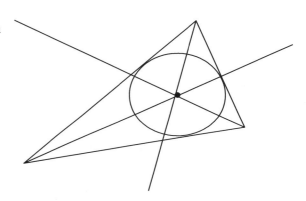

The point where the three angle bisectors intersect is called the incenter. The incenter is equidistant from all three sides of the triangle.

Because each of a triangle's sides is be tangent to an inscribed circle, the circle's radius is perpendicular to each side. Draw a line from the incenter which is perpendicular to one of the triangle's sides. Place the compass tip on the incenter and adjust the width so that two arcs can be drawn on one of the sides of the triangle. Without changing the compass width, place the tip on one of the side-arc intersections and draw an arc outside the triangle; then, place the tip on the other side-arc intersection and draw an arc which intersects the first. Use a straightedge to connect this point of intersection to the incenter.

To draw the circle, position the tip on the compass at the incenter and adjust the compass width to meet the triangle's side where it is crossed by the constructed perpendicular. Draw a circle inside the triangle, noting that the circle touches the triangle once on each side.

Construction of a circle circumscribed around a triangle

Construct the perpendicular bisector of each side of the triangle. Place the compass tip on one of the vertices, open the compass past the middle of the side, and draw an arc that extends both inside and outside the triangle. Without changing the compass opening, move to the other endpoint of the side and draw another arc that intersects the first. Use the straightedge to draw the line that connects the two intersections of the arcs and that is perpendicular to the side it bisects. Repeat these steps for the other two sides of the triangle.

The point where the perpendicular bisectors intersect is called the circumcenter. The circumcenter is equidistant from all three vertices of the triangle. Place the compass tip on the circumcenter and open the compass so the pencil is touching one of the vertices. Draw a circle around the triangle, noting that the circle touches the triangle at each of its vertices.

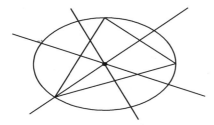

Prove the sum of the measures of opposite angles in a quadrilateral inscribed in a circle is $180°$.

Since quadrilateral $ABCD$ is inscribed in circle P, angles A, B, C, and D are all inscribed in circle P.

The measure of an inscribed angle is equal to half the arc it intercepts. Angle A intercepts $\widehat{BCD}$ and angle C intercepts $\widehat{DAB}$.	$m\angle A = \dfrac{1}{2} \cdot m\widehat{BCD} \;\rightarrow\; m\widehat{BCD} = 2 \cdot m\angle A$ $m\angle C = \dfrac{1}{2} \cdot m\widehat{DAB} \;\rightarrow\; m\widehat{DAB} = 2 \cdot m\angle C$
$\widehat{BCD}$ and $\widehat{DAB}$ are two arcs that form a whole circle.	$m\widehat{BCD} + m\widehat{DAB} = 360°$
Use substitution.	$2 \cdot m\angle A + 2 \cdot m\angle C = 360°$
Use the distributive property and divide by 2.	$2 \cdot (m\angle A + m\angle C) = 360°$ $m\angle A + m\angle C = 180°$

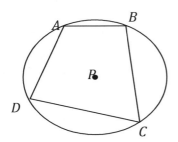

Construct a tangent line from a point outside a circle to the circle.

Consider ⊙ C and a point A outside of circle C. First, use a straightedge to construct $\overline{AC}$. Find M, the midpoint of $\overline{AC}$. Place the compass tip on point M and draw a circle through C. These two points of intersection (points B and D) are both points of tangency. Use a straightedge to construct a line through either point of tangency and point A. This line is tangent to circle C from a point outside the circle.

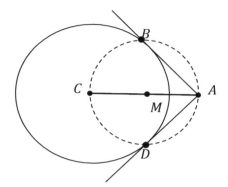

Using similarity to show the length of an arc intercepted by a central angle is proportional to the radius

Consider two concentric circles, ⊙ C with radius r and ⊙ C with radius R. ∠ACB cuts an arc ($\widehat{AB}$) in the larger circle and a similar arc ($\widehat{DE}$) in the smaller circle. The circumference of a circle is $2\pi r$ and an arc is a piece of the circle. The measure of the central angle determines what fraction the arc is of the circle. So, to find the length of the arc, multiply the fraction and the circumference.

In degrees, $l\widehat{AB} = \frac{m\angle C}{360} \cdot 2\pi R$. In radians, $l\widehat{AB} = \frac{m\angle C}{2\pi} \cdot 2\pi R = m\angle C \cdot R$.

In degrees, $l\widehat{DE} = \frac{m\angle C}{360} \cdot 2\pi r$. In radians, $l\widehat{DE} = \frac{m\angle C}{2\pi} \cdot 2\pi r = m\angle C \cdot r$.

Using radians, $\frac{l\widehat{AB}}{R} = m\angle C$ and $\frac{l\widehat{DE}}{r} = m\angle C$, so $\frac{l\widehat{AB}}{R} = \frac{l\widehat{DE}}{r}$. The lengths of the arcs are proportional to the lengths of the radii.

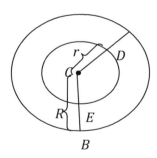

Using similarity to define radian measure of a central angle as the constant of proportionality

Consider two concentric circles, $\odot C$ with radius r and $\odot C$ with radius R. $\angle ACB$ cuts an arc $(\widehat{AB})$ in the larger circle and a similar arc $(\widehat{DE})$ in the smaller circle. The lengths of the arcs are proportional to the lengths of the radii: $\frac{l\widehat{AB}}{R} = \frac{l\widehat{DE}}{r}$.

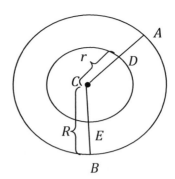

$$l\widehat{AB} = \frac{m\angle C}{2\pi} \cdot 2\pi R = m\angle C \cdot R \;\rightarrow\; \frac{l\widehat{AB}}{R} = m\angle C.$$

$$l\widehat{DE} = \frac{m\angle C}{2\pi} \cdot 2\pi r = m\angle C \cdot r \rightarrow \frac{l\widehat{DE}}{r} = m\angle C.$$

Looking at the equations, $\frac{l\widehat{AB}}{R} = m\angle C$ and $\frac{l\widehat{DE}}{r} = m\angle C$, so the constant of the proportion is the radian measure of angle C.

Deriving the formula for the area of a sector

The area of $\odot C$ is πr^2. A circle has $360°$ and a sector is a slice of the circle. The measure of the central angle determines what fraction the sector is of the circle. So, to find the area of the sector, multiply the fraction and the area of the whole circle.

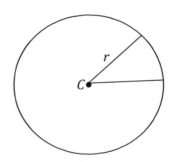

In degrees, $Area_{sector} = \frac{m\angle C}{360} \cdot \pi r^2$.

In radians, $Area_{sector} = \frac{m\angle C}{2\pi} \cdot \pi r^2 = \frac{m\angle C}{2} \cdot r^2$.

Expressing Geometric Properties with Equations

Deriving the equation of a circle with a given center and radius using the Pythagorean Theorem

Given is a circle with center (h, k) and radius r. Point (x, y) is on the circle. Use the Pythagorean Theorem to determine a relationship between the distance r and the points (h, k) and (x, y). In the right triangle, the length of the horizontal leg is $(x - h)$ and the length of the vertical leg is $(y - k)$. The Pythagorean Theorem states that the square of the hypotenuse is equal to the sum of the squares of the legs, or $(x - h)^2 + (y - k)^2 = r^2$. This equation defines the circle with center (h, k), radius r, and point (x, y) on the circle.

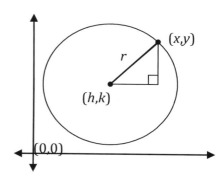

Finding the equation of a circle with center $(-2, 8)$ and radius $r = 6$ using the Pythagorean Theorem

Given a circle with center $(-2, 8)$ and radius $r = 6$. Point (x, y) is on the circle. Use the Pythagorean Theorem to determine a relationship between the distance $r = 6$ and the points $(-2, 8)$ and (x, y). In the right triangle, the length of the horizontal leg is $(x + 2)$ and the length of the vertical leg is $(y - 8)$. The Pythagorean Theorem states that the square of the hypotenuse is equal to the sum of the squares of the legs, or $(x - h)^2 + (y - k)^2 = r^2 \rightarrow (x + 2)^2 + (y - 8)^2 = 6^2 \rightarrow (x + 2)^2 + (y - 8)^2 = 36$.

Use completing the square to find the center and radius of a circle given by the polynomial equation: $x^2 + y^2 + 6x - 2y - 6 = 0$

In a polynomial of the form $Ax^2 + By^2 + Cx + Dy + E = 0$, the equation defines a circle when $A = B$.

	Rewrite the equation by grouping the x-terms and y-terms and moving the constant to the other side of the equation.	$x^2 + y^2 + 6x - 2y - 6 = 0$ $(x^2 + 6x) + (y^2 - 2y) = 6$
	Prepare to complete the square by adding spaces in each set of parentheses and on the other side of the equation.	$(x^2 + 6x + \_) + (y^2 - 2y + \_)$ $= 6 + \_ + \_$
For the x group: $\left(\frac{6}{2}\right)^2 = 3^2 = 9$ For the y group: $\left(\frac{2}{2}\right)^2 = 1^2 = 1$	Determine what is added to each group by dividing the middle coefficient by 2 and then squaring the result.	$(x^2 + 6x + 9) + (y^2 - 2y + 1) = 6 + 9 + 1$
	Factor the groups and simplify the right side of the equation.	$(x + 3)^2 + (y - 1)^2 = 16$
	Identify h, k, and r.	$x - h = x + 3 \rightarrow h = -3$ $y - k = y - 1 \rightarrow k = 1$ $r^2 = 16 \rightarrow r = 4$

The center of the circle is (-3, 1), and the radius is 4.

Identify the equation of a parabola given a focus and directrix

1. focus: (2,5) and directrix: $y = 1$

2. focus: $(6, -2)$ and directrix: $x = 0$

A parabola is the set of points equidistant from a point called the focus and line called the directrix, which does not pass through the focus. A parabola curves around the focus and away from the directrix but intersects neither. The vertex (h, k) of the parabola lies on the parabola's line of symmetry, which passes through the focus and is perpendicular to the directrix.

1. Identify the orientation of the parabola. Since the directrix is a horizontal line represented by the equation $y = 1$, the parabola is oriented vertically and can therefore be represented by the equation $4p(y - k) = (x - h)^2$, where (h, k) is the vertex of the parabola and $(h, k + p)$ is the focus of the parabola. The vertex is halfway between the focus and the directrix, so find the mean of the y-values in the focus and directrix to find the vertex: $\left(2, \frac{5+1}{2}\right) \rightarrow (2,3) = (h, k)$. The y-value of the focus, 5, is represented by $k + p$; $k = 3$, so $3 + p = 5 \rightarrow p = 2$. Substitute h, k, and p into the equation of a parabola: $4p(y - k) = (x - h)^2 \rightarrow 8(y - 3) = (x - 2)^2$.

2. Identify the orientation of the parabola. Since the directrix is a vertical line represented by the equation $x = 0$, the parabola is oriented horizontally and can therefore be represented by the equation $4p(x - h) = (y - k)^2$, where (h, k) is the vertex of the parabola and $(h + p, k)$ is the focus of the parabola. The vertex is halfway between the focus and the directrix, so find the mean of the x-values in the focus and directrix to find the vertex: $\left(\frac{6+0}{2}, -2\right) \rightarrow (3, -2)$. Compare the x-values in the vertex and the focus to find p: $p = 6 - 3 = 3$. Substitute h, k, and p into the equation of a parabola: $4p(x - h) = (y - k)^2 \rightarrow 12(x - 3) = (y + 2)^2$.

Identify the equation of an ellipse with foci at (5,3) and (11,3) and a focal constant of 10

An ellipse is the set of points around two foci such that the sum of the distances from any point on the ellipse to each focus is the focal constant. The center of the ellipse is equidistant from the foci and lies on the major axis. The orientation of the ellipse is also along the major axis. The ends of the major axis are called vertices. The ends of the minor axis are called co-vertices.

Identify the orientation of the ellipse. The y-values are the same in both foci, so the major axis of the ellipse is at $y = 3$. Therefore, the ellipse is oriented horizontally. The equation for an ellipse with a horizontal major axis is $\frac{(x-h)^2}{a^2} + \frac{(y-k)^2}{b^2} = 1$, where (h, k) is the center of the ellipse, a is half the focal constant, and a and b are related by the equation $a^2 - b^2 = c^2$, where c is the horizontal distance between the focus and the center.

The center is the point along the major axis between the two foci: $\left(\frac{11+5}{2}, 3\right) \rightarrow (8,3)$. Find the horizontal distance c between the focus and the center: $c = 11 - 8 = 3$. Divide the focal constant by 2 to find a: $a = \frac{10}{2} = 5$. Find b by using a, c, and the formula $a^2 - b^2 = c^2$: $5^2 - b^2 = 3^2 \rightarrow 25 - b^2 = 9 \rightarrow b^2 = 25 - 9 = 16 \rightarrow b = 4$. Substitute a, b, h, and k into the equation of an ellipse: $\frac{(x-h)^2}{a^2} + \frac{(y-k)^2}{b^2} = 1 \rightarrow \frac{(x-8)^2}{5^2} + \frac{(y-3)^2}{4^2} = 1 \rightarrow \frac{(x-8)^2}{25} + \frac{(y-3)^2}{16} = 1$.

Identify the equation of an ellipse with foci at $(2,1)$ and $(2,5)$ and a focal constant of 5

An ellipse is the set of points around two foci such that the sum of the distances from any point on the ellipse to each focus is the focal constant. The center of the ellipse is equidistant from the foci and lies on the major axis. The orientation of the ellipse is also along the major axis. The ends of the major axis are called vertices. The ends of the minor axis are called co-vertices.

Identify the orientation of the ellipse. The x-values are the same in both foci, so the major axis of the ellipse is at $x = 2$. Therefore, the ellipse is oriented vertically. The equation for an ellipse with a horizontal major axis is $\frac{(x-h)^2}{b^2} + \frac{(y-k)^2}{a^2} = 1$, where (h, k) is the center of the ellipse, a is half the focal constant, and a and b are related by the equation $a^2 - b^2 = c^2$, where c is the vertical distance between the focus and the center.

The center is the point along the major axis between the two foci: $\left(2, \frac{1+5}{2}\right) \rightarrow (2,3)$. Find the vertical distance c between the focus and the center: $c = 5 - 3 = 2$. Divide the focal constant by 2 to find a: $a = \frac{5}{2} = 2.5$. Find b by using a, c, and the formula $a^2 - b^2 = c^2$: $(2.5)^2 - b^2 = 2^2 \rightarrow 6.25 - b^2 = 4 \rightarrow b^2 = 6.25 - 4 = 2.25 \rightarrow b = 1.5$. Substitute a, b, h, and k into the equation of an ellipse: $\frac{(x-h)^2}{b^2} + \frac{(y-k)^2}{a^2} = 1 \rightarrow \frac{(x-2)^2}{1.5^2} + \frac{(y-3)^2}{2.5^2} = 1 \rightarrow \frac{(x-2)^2}{2.25} + \frac{(y-3)^2}{6.25} = 1 \rightarrow \frac{(x-2)^2}{\frac{9}{4}} + \frac{(y-3)^2}{\frac{25}{4}} = 1 \rightarrow \frac{4(x-2)^2}{9} + \frac{4(y-3)^2}{25} = 1$

Identify the equation of a hyperbola given the foci $(-4,5)$ and $(6,5)$ and focal constant 8

A hyperbola is the set of points whose distances from the foci are different by a constant (the focal constant). The foci are two points, one in each section of the hyperbola. The center, (h, k), is a point between the two sections of the hyperbola and is equidistant from the foci and along the major axis.

To find the equation of the hyperbola, first identify the orientation of the hyperbola. The foci lie along the line $y = 5$, so the hyperbola is orientated horizontally. The center is the point equidistant from the foci: $\left(\frac{-4+6}{2}, 5\right) \rightarrow (1,5)$. Compare the x-values of the center and one focus to find c: $c = 1 - (-4) = 5$. Divide the focal constant by 2 to find a: $a = \frac{8}{2} = 4$. Find b by using a, c, and the formula $a^2 + b^2 = c^2$: $4^2 + b^2 = 5^2 \rightarrow 16 + b^2 = 25 \rightarrow b^2 = 25 - 16 = 9 \rightarrow b = 3$. Substitute a, b, h, and k into the equation of a horizontally oriented hyperbola: $\frac{(x-h)^2}{a^2} - \frac{(y-k)^2}{b^2} = 1 \rightarrow \frac{(x-1)^2}{4^2} - \frac{(y-5)^2}{3^2} = 1 \rightarrow \frac{(x-1)^2}{16} - \frac{(y-5)^2}{9} = 1$.

Identify the equation of a hyperbola with foci at $(-2,-4)$ and $(-2, 22)$ and a focal constant of 10

A hyperbola is the set of points whose distances from the foci are different by a constant (the focal constant). The foci are two points, one in each section of the hyperbola. The center, (h, k), is a point between the two sections of the hyperbola and is equidistant from the foci and along the major axis.

To find the equation of the hyperbola, first identify the orientation of the hyperbola. The foci lie along the line $x = -2$, so the hyperbola is orientated vertically. The center is the point equidistant from the foci: $\left(-2, \frac{-4+22}{2}\right) \rightarrow (-2,9)$. Compare the y-values of the center and one focus to find c: $c = 22 - 9 = 13$. Divide the focal constant by 2 to find a: $a = \frac{10}{2} = 5$. Find b by using a, c, and the formula $a^2 + b^2 = c^2$: $5^2 + b^2 = 13^2 \rightarrow 25 + b^2 = 169 \rightarrow b^2 = 169 - 25 = 144 \rightarrow b = 12$. Substitute a, b, h, and k into the equation of a vertically oriented hyperbola: $\frac{(y-k)^2}{a^2} - \frac{(x-h)^2}{b^2} = 1 \rightarrow \frac{(y-9)^2}{5^2} - \frac{(x+2)^2}{12^2} = 1 \rightarrow \frac{(y-9)^2}{25} - \frac{(x+2)^2}{144} = 1$.

Determine whether or not the quadrilateral defined by $A(5,4)$, $B(-4,3)$, $C(-4,1)$, and $D(5,1)$ is a rectangle

A rectangle has two pairs of congruent opposite sides and four right angles. To find the lengths of the sides, use the distance formula, $d = \sqrt{(x_1 - x_2)^2 + (y_1 - y_2)^2}$.

AB	BC
$\sqrt{[5 - (-4)]^2 + (4 - 3)^2}$	$\sqrt{[-4 - (-4)]^2 + (3 - 1)^2}$
$\sqrt{(9)^2 + (1)^2}$	$\sqrt{(0)^2 + (2)^2}$
$\sqrt{81 + 1}$	$\sqrt{0 + 4}$
$\sqrt{82}$	$\sqrt{4} = 2$
CD	DA
$\sqrt{(-4 - 5)^2 + (1 - 1)^2}$	$\sqrt{(5 - 5)^2 + (1 - 4)^2}$
$\sqrt{(-9)^2 + (0)^2}$	$\sqrt{(0)^2 + (-3)^2}$
$\sqrt{81 + 0}$	$\sqrt{0 + 9}$
$\sqrt{81} = 9$	$\sqrt{9} = 3$

Since $AB \neq CD$ and $BC \neq DA$, Quadrilateral $ABCD$ is not a rectangle, and no further testing is required.

Determine whether or not the quadrilateral defined by $A(8, -1)$, $B(-2, -1)$, $C(-2, 6)$, **and** $D(8, 6)$ **is a rectangle**

A rectangle has two pairs of congruent opposite sides and four right angles. To find the lengths of the sides, use the distance formula, $d = \sqrt{(x_1 - x_2)^2 + (y_1 - y_2)^2}$.

AB	BC
$\sqrt{[8 - (-2)]^2 + [-1 - (-1)]^2}$	$\sqrt{[-2 - (-2)]^2 + (-1 - 6)^2}$
$\sqrt{(10)^2 + (0)^2}$	$\sqrt{(0)^2 + (-7)^2}$
$\sqrt{100 + 0}$	$\sqrt{0 + 49}$
$\sqrt{100} = 10$	$\sqrt{49} = 7$
CD	DA
$\sqrt{(-2 - 8)^2 + (6 - 6)^2}$	$\sqrt{(8 - 8)^2 + [6 - (-1)]^2}$
$\sqrt{(-10)^2 + (0)^2}$	$\sqrt{(0)^2 + (7)^2}$
$\sqrt{100 + 0}$	$\sqrt{0 + 49}$
$\sqrt{100} = 10$	$\sqrt{49} = 7$

Since $AB = CD$ and $BC = DA$, Quadrilateral $ABCD$ might be a rectangle, and further testing is required. To determine if the angles are right angles, find the slopes of the four sides. Perpendicular sides will have opposite, inverse slopes.

AB	BC
$m = \dfrac{(-1) - (-1)}{(-2) - 8} = \dfrac{0}{-10} = 0$	$m = \dfrac{6 - (-1)}{(-2) - (-2)} = \dfrac{7}{0} = undef$
CD	DA
$m = \dfrac{6 - 6}{8 - (-2)} = \dfrac{0}{10} = 0$	$m = \dfrac{(-1) - 6}{(-2) - (-2)} = \dfrac{-7}{0} = undef$

Although $\overline{BC}$ and $\overline{DA}$ have undefined slopes, they are perpendicular to $\overline{AB}$ and $\overline{CD}$ because lines with undefined slopes are perpendicular to lines with slopes of 0.

Determine whether or not the point $(3, 3\sqrt{3})$ **lies on the circle which is centered at the origin and which contains the point** $(0, 6)$

To check that a point lies on a circle, find the radius, r, of the circle using the given point and center, (h, k).	$(x - h)^2 + (y - k)^2 = r^2$
	$(0 - 0)^2 + (6 - 0)^2 = r^2$
	$(0)^2 + (6)^2 = r^2$
$x = 0$	$0 + 36 = r^2$
$y = 6$	$36 = r^2$
$h = 0$	$6 = r$
$k = 0$	
Then check to see if the point lies on a circle with the same center and radius.	$(x - h)^2 + (y - k)^2 = r^2$
	$(3 - 0)^2 + \left(3\sqrt{3} - 0\right)^2 = r^2$
$x = 3$	$(3)^2 + \left(3\sqrt{3}\right)^2 = r^2$
$y = 3\sqrt{3}$	$9 + 27 = r^2$
$h = 0$	$36 = r^2$
$k = 0$	$6 = r$

The two circles have the same center $(0,0)$ and the same radius $r = 6$, so both the point $(3,3\sqrt{3})$ lies on the circle which is centered at the origin and which contains the point $(0,6)$.

Determine whether or not the point $(1,2)$ lies on the circle which is centered at the origin and which contains the point $(\sqrt{2}, \sqrt{2})$

To check that a point lies on a circle, find the radius, r, of the circle using the given point and center, (h, k). $$x = \sqrt{2}$$ $$y = \sqrt{2}$$ $$h = 0$$ $$k = 0$$	$$(x - h)^2 + (y - k)^2 = r^2$$ $$(\sqrt{2} - 0)^2 + (\sqrt{2} - 0)^2 = r^2$$ $$(\sqrt{2})^2 + (\sqrt{2})^2 = r^2$$ $$2 + 2 = r^2$$ $$4 = r^2$$ $$2 = r$$
Then check to see if the point lies on a circle with the same center and radius. $$x = 1$$ $$y = 2$$ $$h = 0$$ $$k = 0$$	$$(x - h)^2 + (y - k)^2 = r^2$$ $$(1 - 0)^2 + (2 - 0)^2 = r^2$$ $$(1)^2 + (2)^2 = r^2$$ $$1 + 4 = r^2$$ $$5 = r^2$$ $$\sqrt{5} = r$$

The point $(1,2)$ does not lie on the circle which is centered at the origin and which contains the point $(\sqrt{2}, \sqrt{2})$.

Show that the lines given by equations $5y + 2x = 7$ and $10y + 4x = 28$ are parallel

Parallel lines are two lines which have the same slope and do not intersect. To determine whether $5y + 2x = 7$ and $10y + 4x = 28$ are parallel, first find the slope of each line by rewriting in slope-intercept form: $5y = -2x + 7 \rightarrow y = \frac{-2}{5}x + \frac{7}{5}$; $10y = -4x + 28 \rightarrow y = \frac{-4}{10}x + \frac{28}{10} \rightarrow y = \frac{-2}{5}x + \frac{14}{5}$. The two lines have same slope. To show the lines do not intersect, show that there is no solution to the system formed by the given equations. $\frac{-2}{5}x + \frac{7}{5} = \frac{-2}{5}x + \frac{14}{5} \rightarrow \frac{7}{5} = \frac{14}{5}$. When the solution of a system of equations results in a false statement, the solution is the empty set; there is no point contained by both lines, so the lines do not intersect.

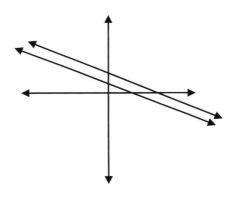

Show that the lines given by equations $y - 3x = 5$ **and** $3y + x = -6$ **are perpendicular**

When two lines have slopes which are negative reciprocals of each other. ($m_1 \cdot m_2 = -1$), they are perpendicular, which means they meet at right angles.

Find the slope of the given two lines, $y - 3x = 5$ and $3y + x = -6$, by rewriting in slope-intercept form: $y = 3x + 5$; $3y = -x - 6 \rightarrow y = \frac{-1}{3}x - \frac{6}{3} \rightarrow y = \frac{-1}{3}x - 2$. The two lines have slopes $m_1 = 3$ and $m_2 = \frac{-1}{3}$, which are negative reciprocals. Therefore, the lines are perpendicular.

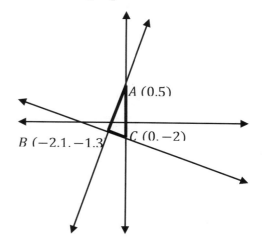

Find the equation of the line passing through $(-2,6)$ **and parallel to** $5y - 15x = -25$

Parallel lines have the same slopes.

Given equation: $5y - 15x = -25$
$$5y = 15x - 25$$
$$y = 3x - 5$$

Slope: $m_1 = 3 = m_2$

Solution equation: $y = m \cdot x + b$
$(y = 6, m_2 = 3, x = -2)$
$$6 = 3 \cdot (-2) + b$$
$$6 = -6 + b$$
$$12 = b$$

$$y = 3x + 12$$
$$y - 3x = 12$$

The line passing through $(-2,6)$ and parallel to $5y - 15x = -25$ is $y - 3x = 12$.

Find the equation of the line passing through $(9, -1)$ **and perpendicular to** $-2y + 3x = 5$

Perpendicular lines have opposite, inverse slopes.

Given equation: $-2y + 3x = 5$
$$-2y = -3x + 5$$
$$y = \frac{-3}{-2}x + 5$$
$$y = \frac{3}{2}x + 5$$

Slope: $m_1 = \frac{3}{2}$
$$m_1 \cdot m_2 = -1$$
$$\frac{3}{2} \cdot m_2 = -1$$
$$m_2 = \frac{-2}{3}$$

Solution equation: $y = m \cdot x + b$
$(y = -1, m_2 = \frac{-2}{3}, x = 9)$
$$-1 = \frac{-2}{3} \cdot 9 + b$$
$$-1 = -6 + b$$
$$5 = b$$

$$y = \frac{-2}{3} \cdot x + 5$$
$$3y = -2x + 15$$
$$3y + 2x = 15$$

The line passing through $(9, -1)$ and perpendicular to $-2y + 3x = 5$ is $3y + 2x = 15$.

Find the point that partitions a given line segment into two segments with a given length ratio.

Given two points, (x_1, y_1) and (x_2, y_2) and the ratio $a:b$.

steps:	x-values:	y-values:
(1) find the difference between the values	$d_x = x_2 - x_1$	$d_y = y_2 - y_1$
(2) find the fraction that represents the ratio	$a:b \rightarrow \dfrac{a}{a+b}$ this is the fraction of difference between x_1 and x_3	$a:b \rightarrow \dfrac{a}{a+b}$ this is also the fraction of difference between y_1 and y_3
(3) find the difference between the first point and the partition point, multiply the fraction and the differences between x_1 and x_2 and y_1 and y_2	$m = \dfrac{a}{a+b} \cdot d_x$	$n = \dfrac{a}{a+b} \cdot d_y$
(4) find the partition point by adding the differences to the first point	$x_3 = x_1 + m$	$y_3 = y_1 + n$

Find the point that partitions the line segment between $(3,4)$ **and** $(7,12)$ **into two segments with a length ratio of** $1:3$

Given two points, $(3,4)$ and $(7,12)$ and ratio $1:3$.

steps:	x-values:	y-values:
(1) find the difference between the values	$d_x = 7 - 3 = 4$	$d_y = 12 - 4 = 8$
(2) find the fraction that represents the ratio	$1:3 \rightarrow \dfrac{1}{1+3} = \dfrac{1}{4}$ this is the fraction of difference between x_1 and x_3	$1:3 \rightarrow \dfrac{1}{1+3} = \dfrac{1}{4}$ this is also the fraction of difference between y_1 and y_3
(3) find the difference between the first point and the partition point, multiply the fraction and the differences between x_1 and x_2 and y_1 and y_2	$m = \dfrac{1}{4} \cdot 4 = 1$	$n = \dfrac{1}{4} \cdot 8 = 2$
(4) find the partition point by adding the differences to the first point	$x_3 = 3 + 1 = 4$	$y_3 = 4 + 2 = 6$

The partition point is $(4,6)$.

Find the point that partitions the line segment between $(-3,5)$ **and** $(3,-7)$ **into two segments with a length ratio of** $5:1$.

Given two points, $(-3,5)$ and $(3,-7)$ and ratio $5:1$.

steps:	x-values:	y-values:
(1) find the difference between the values	$d_x = 3 - (-3) = 6$	$d_y = (-7) - 5 = -12$
(2) find the fraction that represents the ratio	$5:1 \rightarrow \frac{5}{5+1} = \frac{5}{6}$ this is the fraction of difference between x_1 and x_3	$5:1 \rightarrow \frac{5}{5+1} = \frac{5}{6}$ this is also the fraction of difference between y_1 and y_3
(3) find the difference between the first point and the partition point, multiply the fraction and the differences between x_1 and x_2 and y_1 and y_2	$m = \frac{5}{6} \cdot 6 = 5$	$n = \frac{5}{6} \cdot (-12) = -10$
(4) find the partition point by adding the differences to the first point	$x_3 = -3 + 5 = 2$	$y_3 = 5 + (-10) = -5$

The partition point is $(2, -5)$.

Using coordinates to find the perimeter of a figure

Find the distance between all vertices. Add all the distances together.
$$d_{AB} = \sqrt{(x_B - x_A)^2 + (y_B - y_A)^2}$$

Using coordinates to find the area of a figure

Find the critical distances. Use the appropriate formula.

for TRIANGLES:	for RECTANGLES:
find the *BASE* and the *HEIGHT* **the height may not be along the side of the triangle** use the formula: $AREA = \frac{1}{2} \cdot BASE \cdot HEIGHT$	find the *LENGTH* and the *WIDTH* use the formula: $AREA = LENGTH \cdot WIDTH$

Find the perimeter of the figure given by the points $A(5,4)$, $B(3,-1)$, **and** $C(7,-1)$

$d_{AB} = \sqrt{(3-5)^2 + (-1-4)^2} = \sqrt{(-2)^2 + (-5)^2} = \sqrt{4+25} = \sqrt{29}$
$d_{BC} = \sqrt{(7-3)^2 + [-1-(-1)]^2} = \sqrt{(4)^2 + (0)^2} = \sqrt{16+0} = \sqrt{16} = 4$
$d_{CA} = \sqrt{(5-7)^2 + [4-(-1)]^2} = \sqrt{(-2)^2 + (5)^2} = \sqrt{4+25} = \sqrt{29}$
Perimeter: $d_{AB} + d_{BC} + d_{CA} = \sqrt{29} + 4 + \sqrt{29} = 4 + 2\sqrt{29}$.

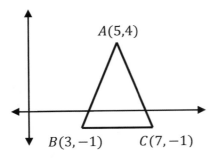

Find the perimeter of the figure given by the points $A(7,11)$, $B(3,3)$, $C(9,0)$ **and** $D(13,8)$

$d_{AB} = \sqrt{(3-7)^2 + (3-11)^2} = \sqrt{(-4)^2 + (-8)^2} = \sqrt{16+64} = \sqrt{80} = 4\sqrt{5}$
$d_{BC} = \sqrt{(9-3)^2 + (0-3)^2} = \sqrt{(6)^2 + (-3)^2} = \sqrt{36+9} = \sqrt{45} = 3\sqrt{5}$
$d_{CD} = \sqrt{(13-9)^2 + (8-0)^2} = \sqrt{(4)^2 + (8)^2} = \sqrt{16+64} = \sqrt{80} = 4\sqrt{5}$
$d_{DA} = \sqrt{(7-13)^2 + (11-8)^2} = \sqrt{(-6)^2 + (3)^2} = \sqrt{36+9} = \sqrt{45} = 3\sqrt{5}$
Perimeter: $d_{AB} + d_{BC} + d_{CD} + d_{DA} = 4\sqrt{5} + 3\sqrt{5} + 4\sqrt{5} + 3\sqrt{5} = 2(4\sqrt{5}) + 2(3\sqrt{5}) = 8\sqrt{5} + 6\sqrt{5} = 14\sqrt{5}$.

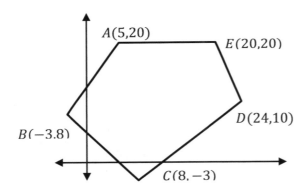

Find the perimeter of the figure given by the points $A(5, 20)$, $B(-3, 8)$, $C(8, -3)$, $D(24, 10)$ and $E(20, 20)$.

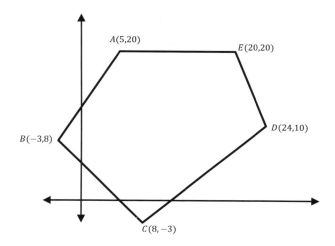

$$d_{AB} = \sqrt{(-3 - 5)^2 + (8 - 20)^2} = \sqrt{(-8)^2 + (-12)^2} = \sqrt{64 + 144} = \sqrt{208} = 4\sqrt{13}$$
$$d_{BC} = \sqrt{[8 - (-3)]^2 + (-3 - 8)^2} = \sqrt{(11)^2 + (-11)^2} = \sqrt{121 + 121} = \sqrt{242} = 11\sqrt{2}$$
$$d_{CD} = \sqrt{(24 - 8)^2 + [10 - (-3)]^2} = \sqrt{(16)^2 + (13)^2} = \sqrt{256 + 169} = \sqrt{425} = 5\sqrt{17}$$
$$d_{DE} = \sqrt{(20 - 24)^2 + (20 - 10)^2} = \sqrt{(-4)^2 + (10)^2} = \sqrt{16 + 100} = \sqrt{116} = 2\sqrt{29}$$
$$d_{EA} = \sqrt{(5 - 20)^2 + (20 - 20)^2} = \sqrt{(-15)^2 + (0)^2} = \sqrt{225 + 0} = \sqrt{225} = 15$$

Perimeter: $d_{AB} + d_{BC} + d_{CD} + d_{DE} + d_{EA} = 4\sqrt{13} + 11\sqrt{2} + 5\sqrt{17} + 2\sqrt{29} + 15$.

Find the area of the figure given by the points $A(5,4)$, $B(3,-1)$, and $C(7,-1)$

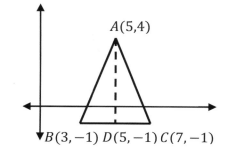

$BASE = d_{BC} = \sqrt{(7 - 3)^2 + [-1 - (-1)]^2} =$
$\sqrt{(4)^2 + (0)^2} = \sqrt{16 + 0} = \sqrt{16} = 4$

The *HEIGHT* is the line segment through A and perpendicular to $\overline{BC}$.

$HEIGHT = d_{AD} = \sqrt{(5 - 5)^2 + (-1 - 4)^2} = \sqrt{(0)^2 + (-5)^2} = \sqrt{0 + 25} = \sqrt{25} = 5$

$AREA = \frac{1}{2} \cdot BASE \cdot HEIGHT = \frac{1}{2} \cdot 4 \cdot 5 = \frac{1}{2} \cdot 20 = 10$

The area of the triangle is 10 square units.

Find the area of the figure given by the points $A(7,11)$, $B(3,3)$, and $C(13,8)$.

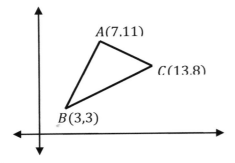

$$BASE = d_{AC} = \sqrt{(13-7)^2 + (8-11)^2} = \sqrt{(6)^2 + (-3)^2} = \sqrt{36+9} = \sqrt{45} = 3\sqrt{5}$$

$\overline{AC} \perp \overline{AB}$ because $m_{AB} \cdot m_{AC} = \frac{11-8}{7-13} \cdot \frac{11-3}{7-3} = \frac{3}{-6} \cdot \frac{8}{4} = \frac{24}{-24} = -1$.

$$HEIGHT = d_{AB} = \sqrt{(3-7)^2 + (3-11)^2} = \sqrt{(-4)^2 + (-8)^2} = \sqrt{16+64} = \sqrt{80} = 4\sqrt{5}$$

$$AREA = \frac{1}{2} \cdot BASE \cdot HEIGHT = \frac{1}{2} \cdot 3\sqrt{5} \cdot 4\sqrt{5} = \frac{1}{2} \cdot 12 \cdot 5 =$$

$$\frac{1}{2} \cdot 60 = 30$$

The area of the triangle is 30 square units.

Find the area of the figure given by the points $A(7,11)$, $B(3,3)$, $C(9,0)$ and $D(13,8)$.

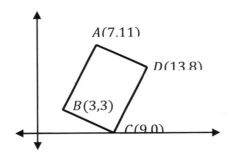

$$LENGTH = d_{AB} = \sqrt{(3-7)^2 + (3-11)^2} = \sqrt{(-4)^2 + (-8)^2} = \sqrt{16+64} = \sqrt{80} = 4\sqrt{5}$$

$\overline{AB} \perp \overline{AD}$ because $m_{AB} \cdot m_{AD} = \frac{11-3}{7-3} \cdot \frac{11-8}{7-13} = \frac{8}{4} \cdot \frac{3}{-6} = \frac{24}{-24} = -1$.

$$WIDTH = d_{AD} = \sqrt{(13-7)^2 + (8-11)^2} = \sqrt{(6)^2 + (-3)^2} =$$
$$\sqrt{36+9} = \sqrt{45} = 3\sqrt{5}$$

$$AREA = LENGTH \cdot WIDTH = 4\sqrt{5} \cdot 3\sqrt{5} = 12 \cdot 5 = 60$$

The area of the rectangle is 60 square units.

- 48 -

Geometric Measurement and Dimension

Formula for the circumference of a circle

Use transformations to show the ratio between the diameter of a circle and the distance around the circle is a constant, π: $\frac{C_{\odot}}{d} = \pi$. As the circle is rotated and translated, the circle moves along the line that is just over three times the length of the diameter.
$C_{\odot} = \pi d = 2\pi r$.

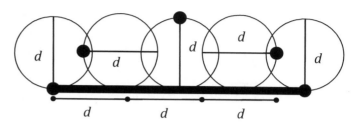

Formula for the area of a circle

Use dissection to show that narrow sectors of the circle can be arranged to fit inside a parallelogram with height r

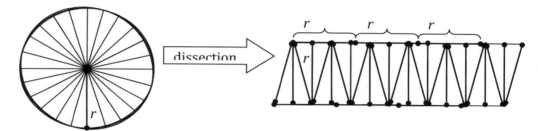

and base πr. Using an informal limit, as the number of sectors increases and approaches a very large number, the dissection becomes more accurate and the difference between the area of the parallelogram and the area of the circle will get smaller.
$A_{\odot} = \pi r^2$.

Formula for the volume of a cylinder

Using Cavalieri's principle, consider a cylinder and all the planes which intersect that cylinder parallel to the base. In each plane, there is a circle congruent to all the other circles in all the other planes. Since the circles are all congruent, they all have the same dimensions and the same areas. When all those circles are stacked together, the resulting solid, the cylinder, has a volume equal to the height of the stack times the area of the base.
$V_{cylinder} = B \cdot h = \pi r^2 h$.

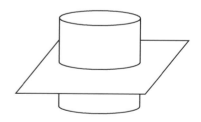

Formula for the volume of a pyramid

Consider a pyramid and a prism with the same altitude and the same base. The area of the prism is $A_{prism} = B \cdot h$ where B is the area of the base and h is the length of the altitude. Notice in the figures, that the pyramid appears to be inside the prism; this indicates that the volume of the pyramid will be less than the volume of the prism. Also notice that there are three different pyramids inside the prism. The first pyramid uses the front vertical edge as its altitude. The second pyramid uses the left vertical edge as its altitude. The third pyramid is the most difficult to see because it is between the other two. The third pyramid uses the right vertical edge as its altitude.

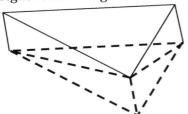 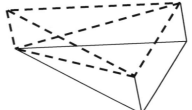 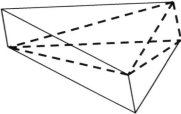

Since there are three pyramids inside the prism, all with the same base and the same altitude, the volume of each pyramid is $\frac{1}{3}$ the volume of the entire prism.

$A_{pyramid} = \frac{1}{3} B \cdot h.$

Formula for the volume of a cone

A pyramid and a cone are similar solids because the cross sections of both become smaller and smaller as they are taken farther and farther from the base.
The volume of a pyramid is $\frac{1}{3} B \cdot h$ where B is the area of the base. If the base of a pyramid is a polygon with n sides, then, using an informal limit, as n increases and approaches a very large number, the shape of the base begins to be like a circle. As shown in the figure to the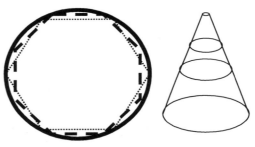
right, even the change from 6 sides to 8 sides makes a much closer approximation of a circle.
So the volume of a cone is also $\frac{1}{3} B \cdot h$ where $B = \pi r^2$.

$V_{cone} = \frac{1}{3} B \cdot h = \frac{1}{3} \pi r^2 h.$

Formula for the volume of a sphere

Consider a cross section of the sphere, not at the center: a circle with radius, c. This circle is a specific distance a from the center of the sphere. These two distances
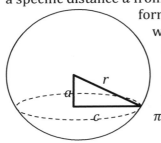 form a right triangle with the radius of the sphere which goes from the center of the sphere to the edge of the circle, so $a^2 + c^2 = r^2$ or $c^2 = r^2 - a^2$. The area of the cross section can be written as a function of the height and radius within the sphere. $A_{cross\ section} = \pi c^2 = \pi(r^2 - a^2) = \pi r^2 - \pi a^2.$

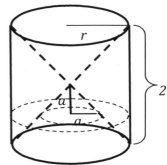

- 50 -

Consider also a cross section of cylinder with from which two congruent cones with tips touching in the cylinder's center have been   removed. Again, let a represent the distance of the cross section's center from the center of the cylinder. The cross section through the cylinder is a circle with radius r from which a circle of radius a has been removed: $A_{cross\ section} = \pi r^2 - \pi a^2$.

Notice that the areas of the cross sections are the same. By Cavalieri's principle, the volumes of the sphere and of the cylinder with cones removed are therefore also the same. The volume of the cylinder without the cones removed is $V = Bh = \pi r^2(2r) = 2\pi r^3$. The volume of each cone is $V = \frac{1}{3}Bh = \frac{1}{3}\pi r^2(r) = \frac{1}{3}\pi r^3$. So, the volume of the cylinder with both cones removed, and therefore the volume of the sphere with radius r, is $2\pi r^3 - 2\left(\frac{1}{3}\pi r^3\right) = \frac{6}{3}\pi r^3 - \frac{2}{3}\pi r^3 = \frac{4}{3}\boldsymbol{\pi r^3}$.

Cavalieri's principle

Cavalieri's principle states that the volumes of two solids are the same if the areas of their corresponding cross sections are equal.

Find the measure of the radius and the height in the cylinder shown if its volume is 603.186 cubic inches.

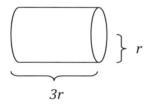

$V_{cylinder} = \pi r^2 h = 603.186$ $h = 3r = 3(4) = 12$
$\pi r^2(3r) = 603.186$
$3\pi r^3 = 603.186$
$\pi r^3 = 201.062$
$r^3 = 64$
$r = 4$

The radius of the cylinder is 4 inches. The height of the cylinder is 12 inches.

Find the volume of the pyramid shown if the base is a square with sides $7\ yds$ **long.**

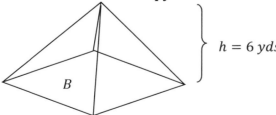

$V_{pyramid} = \frac{1}{3} \cdot Bh = \frac{1}{3} \cdot s^2 h = \frac{1}{3} \cdot 7^2 \cdot 6 = \frac{1}{3} \cdot 49 \cdot 6 = \frac{1}{3} \cdot 294 = 98$

The volume of the pyramid is 98 cubic yards.

Find the amount of batter (in cubic cm) needed to create the ice cream cone shown.

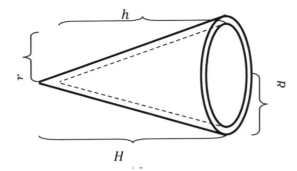

The amount of batter needed is the volume of the solid. The volume is found by subtracting the volume of the inner cone from the volume of the outer cone.

$$V_{outer\ cone} = \frac{1}{3} \cdot \pi R^2 H$$
$$V_{outer\ cone} = \frac{1}{3} \cdot \pi \cdot (2.5)^2 \cdot 10$$
$$V_{outer\ cone} = \frac{1}{3} \cdot \pi \cdot 6.25 \cdot 10$$
$$V_{outer\ cone} = \frac{1}{3} \cdot \pi \cdot 62.5$$
$$V_{outer\ cone} = \pi \cdot 20.833$$
$$V_{outer\ cone} = 65.45$$

$$V_{inner\ cone} = \frac{1}{3} \cdot \pi r^2 h$$
$$V_{inner\ cone} = \frac{1}{3} \cdot \pi \cdot 2^2 \cdot 9.5$$
$$V_{inner\ cone} = \frac{1}{3} \cdot \pi \cdot 4 \cdot 9.5$$
$$V_{inner\ cone} = \frac{1}{3} \cdot \pi \cdot 38$$
$$V_{inner\ cone} = \pi \cdot 12.667$$
$$V_{inner\ cone} = 39.79$$

$$V_{ice\ cream\ cone} = 65.45$$
$$- 39.79$$
$$V_{ice\ cream\ cone} = 25.66$$

25.66 cubic centimeters of batter is needed to create the ice cream cone.

Find the diameter of a sphere, in feet, if the volume of the sphere is 195,432.196 **cubic inches**

$V_{sphere} = \frac{4}{3} \cdot \pi r^3 = 195{,}432.196$ $\pi r^3 = 143{,}574.147$ $r^3 = 46656$ $r = 36$	$d = 2r = 2(36) = 72\ in$ $72\ in \cdot \dfrac{1\ ft}{12\ in} = 6\ ft$

The diameter of the sphere is 6 feet.

Name the vertical, horizontal, and slant cross sections for each of the solids shown

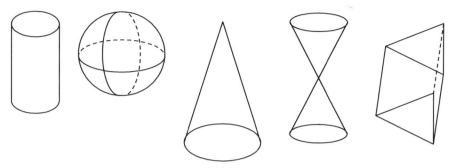

	right cylinder	sphere	right cone	double napped cone	triangular prism
vertical cross section	rectangle	circle	triangle	two triangles	rectangle
horizontal cross section	circle	circle	circle	circle	triangle
slant cross section	figure with two opposite sides parallel and two opposite sides curved	circle	ellipse OR parabola	ellipse OR parabola OR hyperbola	triangle

Name the vertical, horizontal, and slant cross sections for each of the solids shown

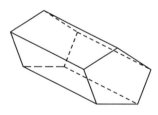 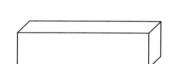 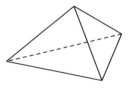

	triangular pyramid	rectangular prism	right pentagonal prism
vertical cross section	triangle	rectangle	pentagon
horizontal cross section	triangle	rectangle	rectangle
slant cross section	quadrilateral OR triangle	rectangle	rectangle

Name the solid created by rotating each of the figures shown around a vertical line through the center of the figure

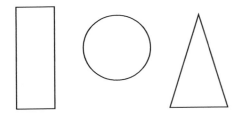

Two dimensional figure	Three-dimensional figure
rectangle	cylinder
circle	sphere
isosceles triangle	cone

Modeling with Geometry

Name geometric shapes that can be used to model the following objects. Describe the properties of the shapes that make it a good model

1. the human torso
2. the human head
3. a coffee mug
4. an iPod
5. a book
6. a tire
7. an apple
8. a piece of string cheese
9. a log

1. The human torso can be modeled using a cylinder. The torso is round with a flat top (shoulders) and a flat bottom (hips).
2. The human head can be modeled using a sphere. The head is round in all directions.
3. A coffee mug can be modeled using a smaller cylinder inside a larger cylinder, aligned at the top. A coffee mug is round with a flat top and bottom.
4. An iPod can be modeled using a shallow rectangular prism. An iPod has two large, flat, rectangular sides (front and back) and four small, rectangular sides (top, bottom, left and right).
5. A book can be modeled on a rectangular prism. A book has six rectangular sides.
6. A tire can be modeled using a smaller cylinder inside a larger cylinder, centered. A tire is round with two flat sides.
7. An apple can be modeled using a sphere. An apple is a round orb.
8. A piece of string cheese can be modeled using a cylinder. A piece of string cheese is round with two flat ends.
9. A log can be modeled using a cylinder. A log is round with two flat ends.

The following table lists the four states with the largest populations in 2010 and the area (in square miles) of each state. Find the population density of each and list the states from highest to lowest population density.

State	2010 Population	Area (square miles)
California	37,253,956	158,648
Texas	25,145,561	266,874
New York	19,378,102	49,112
Florida	18,801,310	58,681

California:
$$\frac{37,253,956}{158,648} \approx 235 \text{ people/sq. mi}$$

Texas:
$$\frac{25,145,561}{266,874} \approx 94 \text{ people/sq. mi}$$

New York:
$$\frac{19,378,102}{49,112} \approx 395 \text{ people/sq. mi}$$

Florida:
$$\frac{18,801,310}{58,681} \approx 320 \text{ people/sq. mi}$$

Highest population density: New York, Florida, California.
Lowest population density: Texas.

The following table lists the four states with the smallest populations in 2010 and the area (in square miles) of each state. Find the population density of each and list the states from highest to lowest population density

State	2010 Population	Area (square miles)
Alaska	710,231	587,878
North Dakota	672,591	70,704
Vermont	625,741	9,615
Wyoming	563,626	97,818

Alaska:

$$\frac{710{,}231}{587{,}878} \approx 1 \text{ person/sq. mi}$$

North Dakota:

$$\frac{672{,}591}{70{,}704} \approx 10 \text{ people/sq. mi}$$

Vermont:

$$\frac{625{,}741}{9{,}615} \approx 65 \text{ people/sq. mi}$$

Wyoming:

$$\frac{563{,}626}{97{,}818} \approx 6 \text{ people/sq. mi}$$

Highest population density: Vermont, North Dakota, Wyoming.

Lowest population density: Alaska.

Salvador needs to determine if a medallion is made of pure gold. He knows the density of gold is 19.3 g/cm^3 and that the medallion weighs 250 g. Salvador submerges the medallion in a cylindrical container of water with a radius of 3 cm. Determine how many centimeters should the water rise to prove the medallion is pure gold

Let x=the volume of a 250 g gold medallion

$$\frac{19.3 \ g}{1 \ cm^3} = \frac{250 \ g}{x \ cm^3}$$
$$19.3 \cdot x = 250 \cdot 1$$
$$x = \frac{250}{19.3}$$
$$x = 12.95$$

The medallion has a volume of 12.95 cm^3 and should therefore displace 12.95cm^3 of water.

h=the change in height of water after medallion added

$$V = \pi r^2 h$$
$$12.95 = \pi \cdot 3^2 \cdot h$$
$$12.95 = 9\pi \cdot h$$
$$0.46 = h$$

The water will rise 0.46 cm if the medallion is made of pure gold.

A lump of metal, part nickel and part copper, weighs 1000 g. Valerie knows the ratio of nickel to copper is $2 : 3$. The density of nickel is 8.89 g/cm^3, and the density of copper is 8.97 g/cm^3. Determine how many centimeters the water will rise when Valerie places the lump into a square prism container of water with sides 6 cm long

Nickel:

Weight: $\frac{2}{5} \cdot 1000 \ g = 400 \ g$

Displacement: $400 \ g \cdot \frac{1 \ cm^3}{8.89 \ g} =$
$44.99 \ cm^3$

Copper:

Weight: $\frac{3}{5} \cdot 1000 \ g = 600 \ g$

Displacement: $600 \ g \cdot \frac{1 \ cm^3}{8.97 \ g} =$
$66.89 \ cm^3$

Total Displacement: 44.99 cm^3 + 66.89 cm^3 =
111.88 cm^3
$$V_s = s^2 \cdot h$$
$$111.88 = 6^2 \cdot h$$
$$111.88 = 36 \cdot h$$
$$3.108 = h$$

The water level will rise 3.108 cm.

A factory cuts large sheets of cardstock (100 in by 102 in) into cards (3 in by 5 in). Determine the maximum number of cards the factory can cut and which side of the cards should be cut from the 100 in side of the sheets

Area of the large sheet: $A_{sheet} = l \cdot w = 100 \cdot 102 = 10200$ square inches	Area of one card: $A_{card} = l \cdot w = 3 \cdot 5 = 15$ square inches	Number of cards made: $\dfrac{10200}{15} = 680$

Option 1: 3 in side cut from 100 in side	Option 2: 5 in side cut from the 100 in side
$\dfrac{100}{3} = 33.3333 \rightarrow 99$ in used and 33 cards per side	$\dfrac{100}{5} = 20 \rightarrow 100$ in used and 20 cards per side
$\dfrac{102}{5} = 20.4 \rightarrow 100$ in used and 20 cards per side	$\dfrac{102}{3} = 34 \rightarrow 102$ in used and 34 cards per side
$33 \cdot 20 = 660$ cards total	$34 \cdot 20 = 680$ cards total

Option 2 should be used to achieve the maximum number of cards made and avoid any wasted material.

A display box is designed to hold a single baseball so the ball touches all six faces of the box. If the diameter of a baseball is 2.9 in, how much empty space is in the box around the ball

$V_{box} = s^3 = 2.9^3 = 24.389$	$V_{space} = V_{box} - V_{ball} = 24.389 - 12.77$
$V_{ball} = \dfrac{4}{3} \cdot \pi r^3 = \dfrac{4}{3} \cdot \pi \cdot (1.45)^3 = 12.77$	$= 11.619$

The box has 11.619 cubic inches of space around the baseball.

Practice Test #1

Practice Questions

1. Which of the following statements is the definition of parallel lines?

Ⓐ Two distinct coplanar lines that intersect at a 90°angle.

Ⓑ Two distinct coplanar lines that do not intersect.

Ⓒ Two rays with a common endpoint that point in opposite directions.

Ⓓ Two rays sharing a common endpoint.

2. The definition "a function that takes points in the plane as inputs and gives other points as outputs" refers to which of the following terms?

Ⓐ Coincident

Ⓑ Invariant

Ⓒ Mensuration

Ⓓ Transformation

3. If trapezoid *JKLM*, shown below, was rotated 180° clockwise about the origin, determine which notation would represent the new coordinates of *J'K'L'M'*?

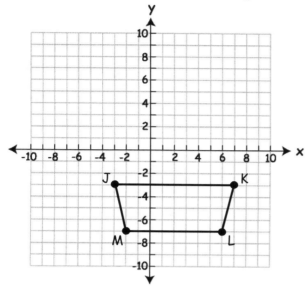

Ⓐ $(x, y) \rightarrow (-x, -y)$

Ⓑ $(x, y) \rightarrow (y, -x)$

Ⓒ $(x, y) \rightarrow (-y, x)$

Ⓓ $(x, y) \rightarrow (y, x)$

4. Which of the following figures show parallelogram *WXYZ* being carried onto its image *W′X′Y′Z′* by a reflection across the *x*-axis?

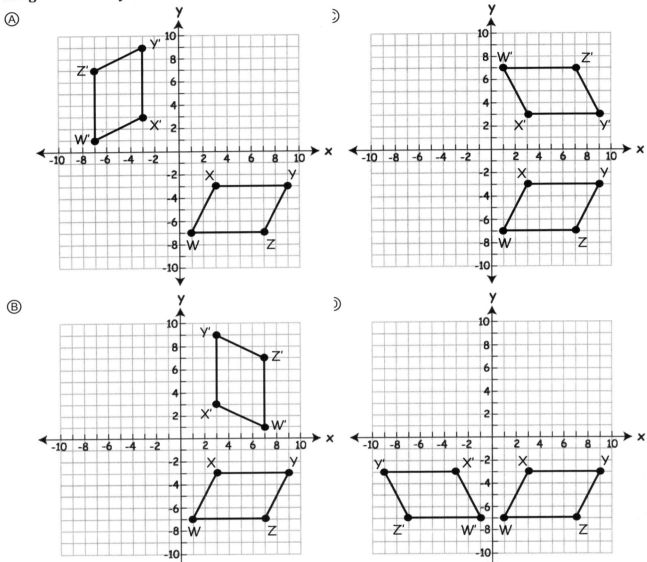

5. If $\overline{ST}$ is reflected across the line $y = x$, what is the new coordinate point of T'?

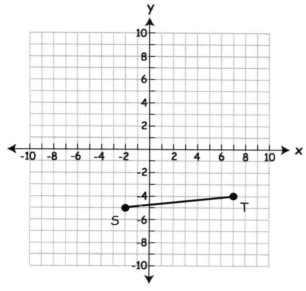

Ⓐ $(7, 4)$

Ⓑ $(-7, -4)$

Ⓒ $(4, -7)$

Ⓓ $(-4, 7)$

6. Which of the following figures has been rotated 90° clockwise about the origin?

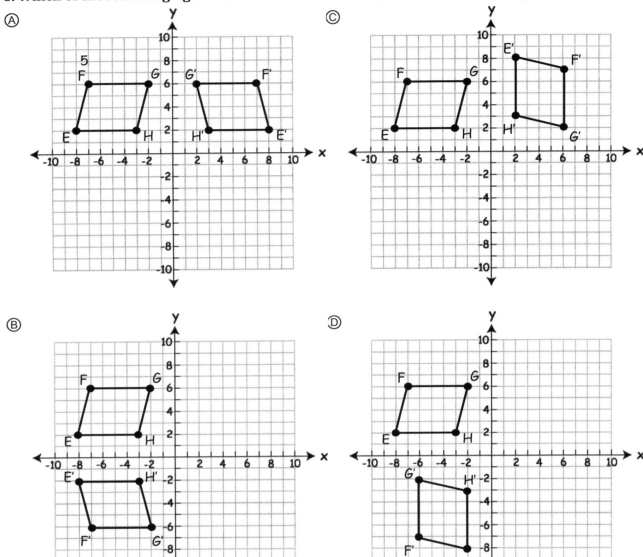

7. Which of the following rules describes the translation of *JKLM* to its image *J'K'L'M'*?

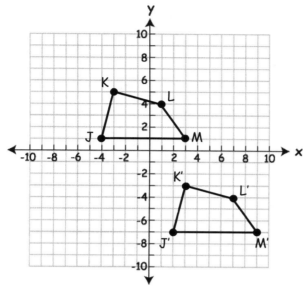

Ⓐ $(x, y) \rightarrow (x - 6, y + 8)$

Ⓑ $(x, y) \rightarrow (x + 6, y - 8)$

Ⓒ $(x, y) \rightarrow (x - 8, y + 6)$

Ⓓ $(x, y) \rightarrow (x + 8, y - 6)$

8. Which set of figures is congruent?

Ⓐ 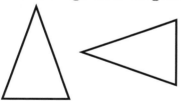   Ⓒ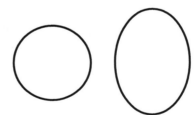

Ⓑ 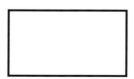   Ⓓ

- 63 -

9. Which of the following is true about the relationship between the two triangles shown below?

 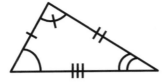

    Ⓐ The triangles are similar.

    Ⓑ The triangles are congruent.

    Ⓒ The triangles are equilateral.

    Ⓓ Both Answer A and Answer B are true.

10. ASA triangle congruence can be used to prove which of the following pairs of triangles congruent?

Ⓐ
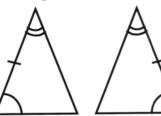

Ⓒ
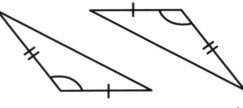

Ⓑ
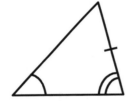

Ⓓ
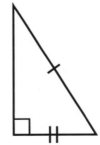 

11. In the figure below, lines *a* and *b* are parallel. Find the value of *x*.

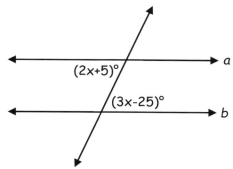

Ⓐ x = 22

Ⓑ x = 30

Ⓒ x = 40

Ⓓ *x* = 65

12. $\overrightarrow{DB}$ is a perpendicular bisector of $\overline{AC}$. If *AB* = 4*x*– 6, *CB* = 2*x* + 2, and *DB* = 6, what is the length of $\overline{AC}$?

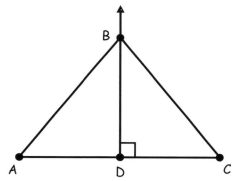

Ⓐ 4

Ⓑ 8

Ⓒ 10

Ⓓ 16

13. Examine the figure below. What is the measure of ∠C?

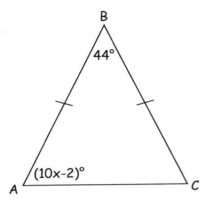

Ⓐ 44°

Ⓑ 68°

Ⓒ 88°

Ⓓ 136°

14. Based on the figure below, if $BG = 6x - 4$ and $GD = 2x + 8$, what is the length of $\overline{GD}$?

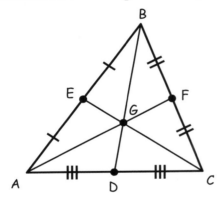

Ⓐ 10

Ⓑ 14

Ⓒ 28

Ⓓ 56

15. In the figure shown below, *ABCD* is a parallelogram.

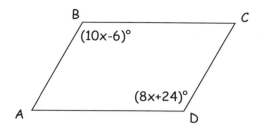

Find the measure of ∠ADC.

Ⓐ 15°

Ⓑ 56°

Ⓒ 96°

Ⓓ 144°

16. The following four steps are needed to bisect a line segment using a compass and straightedge. However, the steps are out of order. Using the numbers listed before each step, identify the correct order of steps for bisecting a line segment.

1 – Without changing the compass width again, set the compass point on the other segment endpoint and draw arcs above and below the segment so that they intersect the previous arcs.

2 – Draw a line segment. Place a compass point on one end of the segment and extend the compass width to be over half of the segment.

3 – Using a straightedge, draw a line between the points where the arcs intersected, which will bisect the line segment.

4 – Without changing the compass width, draw arcs above and below the segment.

Ⓐ 1, 3, 2, 4

Ⓑ 3, 2, 4, 1

Ⓒ 2, 4, 1, 3

Ⓓ 4, 1, 3, 2

- 67 -

17. Examine the following steps:
Step 1 – Using a compass, draw a circle.
Step 2 – Keeping the radius of the compass fixed, mark a point on the circle.
Step 3 – Centered at that point, draw an arc across the circle and mark a point at that intersection.
Step 4 – Center the compass at that new point, draw another arc across the circle and mark that point.
Step 5 – Continue drawing arcs along the circle until there are six points.
Step 6 – Using a straightedge, connect every other point.

The previous steps describe the construction of which shape inscribed in a circle?

Ⓐ Equilateral Triangle

Ⓑ Regular Hexagon

Ⓒ Regular Pentagon

Ⓓ Square

18. If rectangle $ABCD$ is dilated by a scale factor of $\frac{1}{2}$ to create its image $A'B'C'D'$, how does the slope of $\overleftrightarrow{AC}$ compare to the slope of $\overleftrightarrow{A'C'}$?

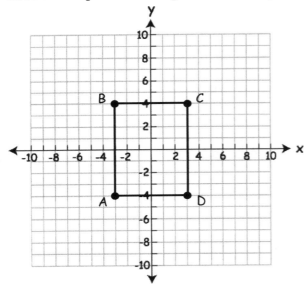

Ⓐ The slope of $\overleftrightarrow{A'C'}$ is half the slope of $\overleftrightarrow{AC}$.

Ⓑ The slope of $\overleftrightarrow{A'C'}$ is double the slope of $\overleftrightarrow{AC}$.

Ⓒ The slope of $\overleftrightarrow{A'C'}$ is the same as the slope of $\overleftrightarrow{AC}$.

Ⓓ The slope of $\overleftrightarrow{A'C'}$ is the reciprocal of the slope of $\overleftrightarrow{AC}$.

19. If $\overline{PQ}$, shown below, is dilated by a scale factor of 4, what are the new coordinates of Q'?

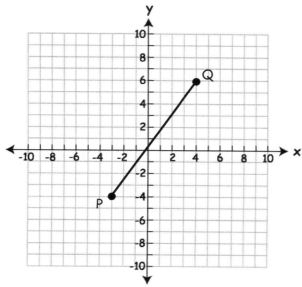

Ⓐ (16, 24)

Ⓑ (8, 10)

Ⓒ (1, 1.5)

Ⓓ (0, 2)

20. Which pair of figures below is similar?

Ⓐ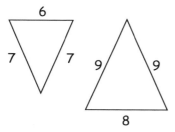

Ⓒ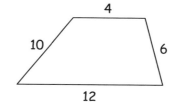

Ⓑ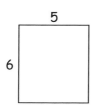

Ⓓ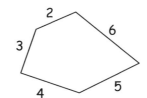

21. Examine the triangles below.

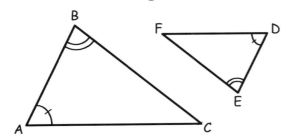

Which of the following theorems can be used to prove that ΔABC~ΔDEF?

Ⓐ AA

Ⓑ ASA

Ⓒ SAS

Ⓓ SSS

22. Given the figure below and that $a = 6$ and $b = 8$, solve for the values x and h.

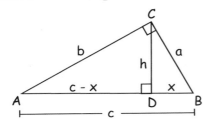

Ⓐ $x = 3.6$ and h $= 4.8$

Ⓑ x $= 4.8$ and h $= 5.2$

Ⓒ x $= 2.4$ and h $= 3.2$

Ⓓ x $= 10$ and $h = 3.2$

23. In the figure below, △ABC≅△DEF.

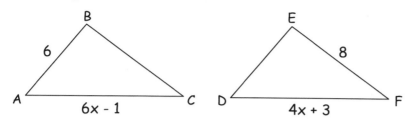

Find the perimeter of △DEF.

Ⓐ 16

Ⓑ 19

Ⓒ 21

Ⓓ 25

24. In △ABC, cos A =

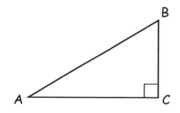

Ⓐ $\frac{AC}{AB}$

Ⓑ $\frac{AC}{BC}$

Ⓒ $\frac{BC}{AC}$

Ⓓ $\frac{BC}{AB}$

25. Sin 38° is equivalent to which of the following values?

Ⓐ sin 142°

Ⓑ sin 52°

Ⓒ cos 52°

Ⓓ cos 38°

26. A 600 m tall radio tower uses 720 m long guide wires for support, as shown in the figure below.

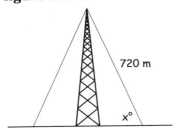

What is the measure of the angle between the ground and the guide wire, as denoted by *x*?

Ⓐ 33.6°

Ⓑ 39.8°

Ⓒ 50.2°

Ⓓ 56.4°

27. A bird sits on top of a 15 ft tall lamp post. Looking down at a 35° angle of depression, the bird sees a bug on the ground. How far is the bug from the base of the lamp post?

Ⓐ 10.5 ft

Ⓑ 18.3 ft

Ⓒ 21.4 ft

Ⓓ 26.2 ft

28. Which of the following formulas can be used to find the area of the triangle shown below?

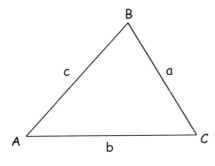

Ⓐ $A = \frac{1}{2}ab\sin(C)$

Ⓑ $A = \frac{1}{2}ab\sin(B)$

Ⓒ $A = \frac{1}{2}bc\sin(B)$

Ⓓ $A = \frac{1}{2}ac\sin(C)$

29. Based on ΔABC below, what is the value of x?

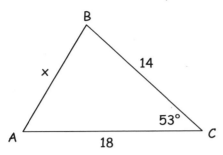

    Ⓐ 10.8

    Ⓑ 11.3

    Ⓒ 14.7

    Ⓓ 22.8

30. Sidney and Robert drive to school each school day. The following map shows the locations of Sidney's house and Robert's house in relation to the school.

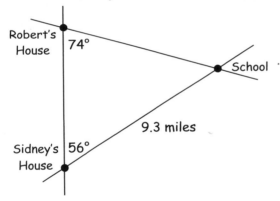

Based on the information in the map, how far does Robert have to drive to get to school in the morning?

    Ⓐ 7.0 miles

    Ⓑ 8.0 miles

    Ⓒ 10.8 miles

    Ⓓ 18.9 miles

31. Which of the following ratios can be used to prove that all circles are similar?

- (A) $\dfrac{\text{Area}}{\text{Circumference}}$
- (B) $\dfrac{\text{Circumference}}{\text{Diameter}}$
- (C) $\dfrac{\text{Radius}}{\text{Area}}$
- (D) $\dfrac{\text{Area}}{\text{Radius}}$

32. $\overline{AB}$ is tangent to Circle O. Find the length of $\overline{OB}$.

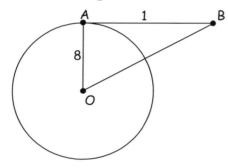

- (A) 13
- (B) 16
- (C) 17
- (D) 23

33. Quadrilateral *ABCD* is inscribed in Circle O.

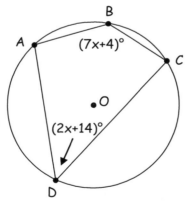

What is the measure of ∠ADC?

- (A) 18°
- (B) 30°
- (C) 50°
- (D) 90°

34. The sides of quadrilateral *PQRS* are tangent to the circle. What is the perimeter of quadrilateral *PQRS*?

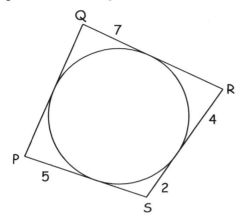

    Ⓐ 36

    Ⓑ 30

    Ⓒ 24

    Ⓓ 18

35. Examine Circle Q below.

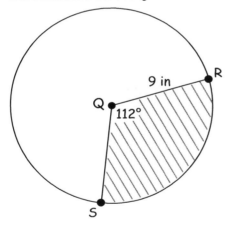

What is the area of sector QRS?

    Ⓐ 17.6 in²

    Ⓑ 79.2 in²

    Ⓒ 254.5 in²

    Ⓓ 316.7 in²

36. A circle is centered at (–5, 3) with a radius of 4. Which of the following equations describes that circle?

Ⓐ $(x - 5)^2 + (y + 3)^2 = 4$

Ⓑ $(x + 5)^2 + (y - 3)^2 = 4$

Ⓒ $(x - 5)^2 + (y + 3)^2 = 16$

Ⓓ $(x + 5)^2 + (y - 3)^2 = 16$

37. Which of the following equations represents a parabola with focus (2, 3) and directrix $y = -1$?

Ⓐ $(y - 1)^2 = 8(x - 2)$

Ⓑ $(y - 3)^2 = -4(x - 2)$

Ⓒ $(x - 2)^2 = 8(y - 1)$

Ⓓ $(x - 2)^2 = -4(y - 3)$

38. Which of the following equations represents an ellipse with foci (–2, 3) and (4, 3) and the sum of the distances from the foci to a point on the ellipse is 8?

Ⓐ $\frac{(x-1)^2}{7} + \frac{(y-3)^2}{16} = 1$

Ⓑ $\frac{(x-1)^2}{16} + \frac{(y-3)^2}{7} = 1$

Ⓒ $\frac{(x-1)^2}{55} + \frac{(y-3)^2}{64} = 1$

Ⓓ $\frac{(x-1)^2}{64} + \frac{(y-3)^2}{55} = 1$

39. A circle centered at (3, 0) passes through the point (7, 0). Which of the following points also lies on the circle?

Ⓐ $(0, 5)$

Ⓑ $(1, 2\sqrt{5})$

Ⓒ $(2, \sqrt{17})$

Ⓓ $(6, \sqrt{7})$

40. Given the line $y = \frac{2}{3}x + 4$, find the equation of a line perpendicular to that line and that passes through the point (6, 2).

Ⓐ $y = \frac{2}{3}x - 2$

Ⓑ $y = -\frac{2}{3}x + 6$

Ⓒ $y = \frac{3}{2}x - 7$

Ⓓ $y = -\frac{3}{2}x + 11$

41. Given points *A* and *B* on a number line, where *A* = –3 and *B* = 7, find point *C*, located between *A* and *B*, such that *C* is four times farther from *A* than it is from *B*.

    Ⓐ –1

    Ⓑ 1

    Ⓒ 3

    Ⓓ 5

42. On a coordinate grid, rectangle *ABCD* has the following coordinates: *A*(–2, 7), *B*(5, 7), *C*(5, –1), and *D*(–2, –1). What is the area of rectangle *ABCD*?

    Ⓐ 18 units^2

    Ⓑ 20 units^2

    Ⓒ 30 units^2

    Ⓓ 56 units^2

43. Which method listed below uses a regular polygon inscribed in a circle to derive the formula for the area of a circle?

    Ⓐ Dissection Argument

    Ⓑ Informal Limits Argument

    Ⓒ Inscribed Angle Theorem

    Ⓓ Pythagorean Theorem

44. In a comparison of two spheres, it is determined that all corresponding cross sections of the spheres have the same area. Based on Cavalieri's principle, what can be said about these two spheres?

    Ⓐ They have the same mass.

    Ⓑ They have the same volume.

    Ⓒ They have the same weight.

    Ⓓ They have the same density.

45. A farmer installed a new grain silo on his property in preparation for the fall harvest. If the silo is in the shape of a cylinder with a diameter of 8 m and a height of 24 m, how much grain will the farmer be able to store in the silo?

Ⓐ 402.1 m³

Ⓑ 1,206.4 m³

Ⓒ 1,608.5 m³

Ⓓ 4,825.5 m³

46. Jack works at an ice cream shop. While placing an order, a customer asked for a sugar cone to be filled in completely level with ice cream before adding any scoops of ice cream on top. If the sugar cone has a diameter of 5 cm and it is 12.5 cm tall, how much ice cream will Jack use to fill the inside of the sugar cone?

Ⓐ 81.8 cm3

Ⓑ 245.4 cm3

Ⓒ 327.2 cm3

Ⓓ 981.7 cm³

47. If a horizontal cross-section was taken of the following triangular prism, what would be the resulting two-dimensional shape?

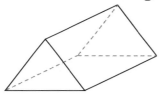

Ⓐ Rectangle

Ⓑ Trapezoid

Ⓒ Triangle

Ⓓ Square

48. The Great Pyramid of Khufu, located in Egypt, is the largest pyramid in the world. In the shape of a square pyramid, the Great Pyramid of Khufu has a height of 481 ft and the length of each side of the base is 756 ft. What is the volume of the Great Pyramid of Khufu?

Ⓐ 1.21×105 ft³

Ⓑ 4.85×105 ft³

Ⓒ 9.16×107 ft³

Ⓓ 2.75×10^8 ft³

49. The city of Minneapolis, Minnesota covers 54.9 square miles of land and has a population of 382,578. What is the population density of Minneapolis?

Ⓐ 126.9 persons/square mile

Ⓑ 6,968.6 persons/square mile

Ⓒ 4,533,532.2 persons/square mile

Ⓓ 248,890,917.9 persons/square mile

50. Zack is building a sand box for his children. A local home improvement store sells bags of sand for \$3.75/bag and each bag contains 0.5 cubic feet of sand. If the sand box has the dimensions 6 ft × 4 ft × 1 ft, how much will it cost Zack to completely fill the sand box with sand?

Ⓐ \$24

Ⓑ \$45

Ⓒ \$90

Ⓓ \$180

Answers and Explanations

Math.Content.G.CO.1

1. B: Parallel lines are two distinct lines in the same plane that do not intersect. Answer A is the definition of perpendicular lines. Answer C is the definition of opposite rays, which form a line. Answer D is the definition of an angle.

Math.Content.G.CO.2

2. D: A transformation is described as a function that takes points in the plane as inputs and gives other points as outputs. In Answer A, coincident means that two images are superimposed on one another. In Answer B, invariant means a property that cannot be changed by a given transformation. In Answer C, mensuration is the measurement of geometric figures, such as length, area, angle measure and volume.

Math.Content.G.CO.3

3. A: A 180° clockwise rotation about the origin takes the original coordinates and negates them. Therefore, the original coordinates of (x, y) become $(-x, -y)$ after the rotation. Answer B is the coordinate change after a 90° clockwise rotation about the origin. Answer C is the coordinate change after a 90° counterclockwise rotation about the origin. Answer D is the Answer B is the coordinate change after a reflection across the line $y = x$.

Math.Content.G.CO.3

4. C: A reflection is a transformation producing a mirror image. A figure reflected over the x-axis will have its vertices in the form (x, y) transformed to $(x, -y)$. The point W at (1,-7) reflects to W' at (1,7). Only Answer C shows $WXYZ$ being carried onto its image $W'X'Y'Z'$ by a reflection across the x-axis. Answer A shows a reflection across the line $y = x$. Answer B shows a 90° counterclockwise rotation about the origin. Answer D shows a reflection across the y-axis.

Math.Content.G.CO.4

5. D: For a reflection across the line $y = x$, the original coordinate points of (x, y) reverse to become (y, x) for the image. Therefore, since T is located at $(7, -4)$, the coordinates of T' after the reflection across the line $y = x$ become $(-4, 7)$. Answer A is for a reflection across the x-axis. Answer B is for a reflection across the y-axis. Answer C is for a 90° clockwise rotation about the origin.

Math.Content.G.CO.5

6. C: Since $EFGH$ is initially located in Quadrant II, a 90° clockwise rotation will rotate the image into Quadrant I. As $EFGH$ is rotated 90° clockwise, each vertex of the figure will undergo the coordinate transition of $(x, y) \rightarrow (y, -x)$, as is the case in Answer C. Answer A is a reflection across the y-axis. Answer B is a reflection across the x-axis. Answer D is a 90° counterclockwise rotation.

Math.Content.G.CO.5

7. B: To determine the translation, compare the coordinates of $J(-4, 1)$ and $J'(2, -7)$. To find the change in the x-direction, subtract the x coordinate of the starting position from the final position that is $\Delta x = 2 - (-4) = 2 + 4 = 6$. Similarly, the change in the y-direction is $-7 - 1 = -8$. We can check that the same is true for the other vertices. Therefore, the rule that describes the translation of $JKLM$ to its image $J'K'L'M'$ is $(x, y) \rightarrow (x + 6, y - 8)$.

Answer A incorrectly used the opposite signs. Answer C incorrectly used the opposite signs and had the *x* and *y* directions reversed. Answer D had the *x* and *y* directions reversed.

Math.Content.G.CO.6

8. A: In order for two figures to be congruent, they must have the same size and shape. The two triangles in Answer A have the same size and shape, even though the second triangle is rotated counterclockwise compared to the first triangle. The rectangles in Answer B are the same shape, but they are not the same size. In Answer C, the second circle has been vertically stretched, so the figures are not the same shape or size. In Answer D, the second trapezoid has been horizontally stretched so it is not the same size as the first trapezoid.

Math.Content.G.CO.7

9. D: Since the two triangles have all three corresponding pairs of sides and corresponding pairs of angles marked congruent, then the two triangles are congruent. Similar triangles are the same shape but not necessarily the same size; they have congruent angles. All congruent triangles are similar triangles, so Answer D is the best choice. In Answer C, equilateral triangles are triangles that have sides with all the same measure within the same triangle, not in relation to another triangle.

Math.Content.G.CO.8

10. A: In order for triangles to be congruent by ASA, there needs to be two pairs of congruent corresponding angles and then the pair of sides between those angles is also congruent. The triangles in Answer A meet the requirements for ASA triangle congruence. In Answer B, the triangles are congruent by AAS. In Answer C, the triangles are congruent by SAS. In Answer D, the triangles are congruent by HL (Hypotenuse Leg).

Math.Content.G.CO.9

11. B: The listed angles are located in the alternate interior angles position. According to the Alternate Interior Angle Theorem, when a transversal cuts across parallel lines, the alternate interior angles are congruent. Since lines *a* and *b* are parallel, it means that $2x + 5 = 3x - 25$. After subtracting $2x$ from both sides and adding 25 to both sides, the equation simplifies as $30 = x$. In Answer A, the angles were incorrectly treated as complementary. In Answer C, the angles were incorrectly treated as supplementary. Answer D is the measure of each alternate interior angle, but the question only wanted the value of *x*.

Math.Content.G.CO.9

12. D: The Perpendicular Bisector Theorem states that the points on a perpendicular bisector of a line segment are exactly those equidistant from the segment's endpoints. Since the point B lies on $\overrightarrow{DB}$, the perpendicular bisector of $\overline{AC}$, it means that the point B is equidistant from both A and C, giving us $AB = CB$. Therefore, $4x - 6 = 2x + 2$. After subtracting $2x$ from both sides and adding 6 to both sides, the equation simplifies as $2x = 8$. Divide both sides by 2 to get $x = 4$. Substituting for *x*, $AB = 4(4) - 6 = 16 - 6 = 10$ and $CB = 2(4) + 2 = 10$. The question asks for the length of $\overline{AC}$, which is the base of $\triangle ABC$. Since $\overrightarrow{DB}$ is a perpendicular bisector, it divides $\triangle ABC$ into two right triangles in which the length of $\overline{AD}$ equals the length of $\overline{DC}$. Since we know that $AB = 10$ and $DB = 6$, we can use the Pythagorean Theorem to find the length of $\overline{AD}$: $(AD)^2 + (DB)^2 = (AB)^2$, $(AD)^2 + 6^2 = 10^2$, $(AD)^2 + 36 = 100$. Subtract 36 from both sides to get $(AD)^2 = 64$. Take the square root of both sides to get $AD = 8$. Since AD is half the length of AC, $AC = 2(8) = 16$. Answer A is the value of *x*. Answer B is the length for each $\overline{AD}$ and $\overline{DC}$. Answer C is the length for each $\overline{AB}$ and $\overline{CB}$.

Math.Content.G.CO.10

13. B: According to the Triangle Sum Theorem, the measures of the three angles in a triangle sum to 180°. Therefore, in the triangle shown, $m\angle A + m\angle B + m\angle C = 180°$. However, we are not initially given the measure of $\angle C$. But, since the triangle is isosceles, the Isosceles Triangle Theorem states that in an isosceles triangle, the base angles (or angles opposite the congruent sides) are congruent. So, in this triangle, $m\angle A = m\angle C$. By substitution, the angle measure equation becomes $10x - 2 + 44 + 10x - 2 = 180$. Simplifying the left side of the equation becomes $20x + 40 = 180$. After subtracting 40 from both sides, the equation becomes $20x = 140$. Finally, divide both sides by 20 to get $x = 7$. Then, substitute that value for x into the expression for the measure of $\angle C$: $10(7) - 2 = 70 - 2 = 68°$. Answer A incorrectly assumed that the $\angle B$ and $\angle C$ were the congruent angles in the isosceles triangle. Answer C incorrectly doubled the measure of $\angle B$. Answer D incorrectly set up the equation as $10x - 2 + 44 = 180$ to get the angle measure of 136°.

Math.Content.G.CO.10

14. C: In $\triangle ABC$, the midpoints are marked as D, E, and F. The medians of the triangle are then drawn in as $\overline{AF}$, $\overline{BD}$ and $\overline{CE}$. The medians intersect at a point called the centroid. Based on this intersection, it is the case that $AG = 2GF$, $BG = 2GD$, and $CG = 2GE$. Since we are given that $BG = 6x - 4$ and $GD = 2x + 8$, we can set up the equation as $6x - 4 = 2(2x + 8)$. Simplifying that equation, it becomes $6x - 4 = 4x + 16$. After subtracting $4x$ from both sides and adding 4 to both sides, the equation becomes $2x = 20$. Divide both sides by 2 to get $x = 10$. Then, the length of $\overline{GD}$ is calculated as $2(10) + 8 = 20 + 8 = 28$. Answer A is the value of x. Answer B is the length of $\overline{GD}$ if the equation was incorrectly set up as $BG = GD$. Answer D is the length of $\overline{BG}$.

Math.Content.G.CO.11

15. D: One of the theorems about parallelograms states that the opposite angles in a parallelogram are congruent. Therefore, according to the figure, $\angle ABC \cong \angle ADC$, so $m\angle ABC = m\angle ADC$. By substitution, that equation becomes $10x - 6 = 8x + 14$. After subtracting $8x$ from both sides and adding 6 to both sides, the equation simplifies as $2x = 30$. Divide both sides by 2 to get $x = 15$. To find the measure of $\angle ADC$, substitute the value for x into the expression for $\angle ADC$: $8(15) + 24 = 120 + 24 = 144°$. Answer A is just the value of x. Answer B is the measure of $\angle ADC$ if the angles were incorrectly thought to be complementary angles. Answer C is the measure of $\angle ADC$ is the angles were incorrectly thought to be supplementary angles.

Math.Content.G.CO.12

16. C: The correct sequence of steps for bisecting a line segment is 2, 4, 1, 3.

Math.Content.G.CO.13

17. A: The listed steps describe the construction of an equilateral triangle inscribed in a circle. If every point was connected using a straightedge, that would have constructed a regular hexagon instead.

Math.Content.G.SRT.1a

18. C: Since rectangle $ABCD$ is centered at the origin and $\overleftrightarrow{AC}$ passes through the origin, any dilation of rectangle $ABCD$ will leave that line unchanged. Since A has the coordinates (−3 −

4) and C has the coordinates (3, 4), the slope of $\overleftrightarrow{AC} = \frac{4-(-4)}{3-(-3)} = \frac{8}{6} = \frac{4}{3}$. When rectangle $ABCD$ is dilated by a scale factor of $\frac{1}{2}$ to create image $A'B'C'D'$, A' has the coordinates (−1.5, −2) and C' has the coordinates (1.5, 2). The slope of $\overleftrightarrow{A'C'} = \frac{2-(-2)}{1.5-(-1.5)} = \frac{4}{3}$. Therefore, the slope of $\overleftrightarrow{A'C'}$ is the same as the slope of $\overleftrightarrow{AC}$.

Math.Content.G.SRT.1b

19. A: If $\overline{PQ}$ is dilated by a scale factor of 4, then the coordinates of P and Q are each multiplied by 4. For point Q, (4, 6) then becomes (16, 24) to get Q'. Answer B results if 4 were added to the coordinates. Answer C results if the coordinates were divided by 4. Answer D results if 4 were subtracted from the coordinates.

Math.Content.G.SRT.2

20. C: In order for figures to be similar, all sets of corresponding sides need to be proportional. All corresponding sides in Answer C are at a 2:1 ratio. In Answer A, the corresponding sides are 2 more for the second figure, instead of being 2 times larger. In Answer B, one set of corresponding sides is at a 1:2 ratio, while the other set of corresponding sides is at a 2:1 ratio. In Answer D, the corresponding sides are 3 more for the second figure, instead of being 3 times larger.

Math.Content.G.SRT.3

21. A: Given the measure of two angles of a triangle, we can find the measure of the remaining angle by the relationship $m\angle BCA = 180° - (m\angle ABC + m\angle CAB)$. Since each triangle shows two pairs of congruent corresponding angles, we know the third pair of angles must be congruent as well. Since all 3 pairs of corresponding angles are congruent, $\triangle ABC$ is similar to $\triangle DEF$. This is known as the AA Similarity Theorem.

Math.Content.G.SRT.4

22. A: Noticing that $\angle BCD$ and $\angle CAD$ are both complimentary to $\angle ACD$, we have that $m\angle BCD = m\angle CAD = m\angle CAB$. By Angle Angle similarity, we know these are similar triangles. By the Pythagorean theorem, $c = \sqrt{a^2 + b^2} = \sqrt{6^2 + 8^2} = 10$. Because ACB is similar to CBD, we have the ratio $\frac{h}{a} = \frac{b}{c}$. Solving for h yields $h = \frac{ab}{c} = \frac{6*8}{10} = 4.8$. Similarly, consider the ratio $\frac{x}{a} = \frac{a}{c}$ and solve for x, giving $x = \frac{a^2}{c} = \frac{(6)^2}{10} = 3.6$.

Math.Content.G.SRT.5

23. D: In order to find the perimeter of $\triangle DEF$, we need to know the values of all three sides of the triangle. We are given that $EF = 8$. Since $\triangle ABC \cong \triangle DEF$, then $DE = AB$, which means that $DE = 6$ as well. Also, since $\triangle ABC \cong \triangle DEF$, then $AC = DF$. Therefore, $6x - 1 = 4x + 3$. After subtracting $4x$ from both sides and adding 1 to both sides, the equation becomes $2x = 4$. Divide both sides by 2 to get $x = 2$. After substituting for x, the value of DF becomes $4(2) + 3 = 8 + 3 = 11$. The perimeter of $\triangle DEF$ then becomes $6 + 8 + 11 = 25$. In Answer A, after solving for x, the value of 2 was incorrectly used for the length of $\overline{DF}$ instead of substituting that value into the $4x + 3$ expression to get the side length. In Answer B, only the sides 8 and 11 were added. In Answer C, after setting up the equation as $6x - 1 = 4x + 3$, although $4x$ was correctly subtracted from both sides, 1 was incorrectly subtracted instead of added to both sides and the equation was incorrectly simplified as $2x = 2$ which results in $x = 1$. Then, $4(1) + 3 = 7$.which leads to an incorrect perimeter of $6 + 8 + 7 = 21$.

- 83 -

Math.Content.G.SRT.6

24. A: The cosine function is represented by the ratio $\frac{adjacent\ leg}{hypotenuse}$. In $\triangle ABC$, the adjacent leg to $\angle A$ is AC and the hypotenuse is AB. Therefore, $\cos A = \frac{AC}{AB}$. Answer B is $\cot A$. Answer C is $\tan A$. Answer D is $\sin A$.

Math.Content.G.SRT.7

25. C: The sine of one angle is equivalent to the cosine of the complementary angle. Therefore, since $90° - 38° = 52°$, then $\sin 38° = \cos 52°$. In Answer A, $142°$ is the supplementary angle to $38°$, but it needs to be the complementary angle. Answer B is the complementary angle, but it is in terms of sine instead of cosine. Answer D is the cosine but the same angle instead of the complementary angle.

Math.Content.G.SRT.8

26. D: The radio tower, the guide wire, and the ground form a right triangle. The guide wire forms the hypotenuse and the radio tower forms the leg opposite of angle x. Therefore, in order to solve for the measure of angle x, it needs to be set up as $\sin x = \frac{opposite\ leg}{hypotenuse}$ or $\sin x = \frac{600}{720}$. The value of x is found using the calculation $x = \sin^{-1}\left(\frac{600}{720}\right) = 56.4°$. Answer A incorrectly used $\cos x = \frac{600}{720}$. Answer B incorrectly used $\tan x = \frac{600}{720}$. Answer C incorrectly used $\tan x = \frac{720}{600}$.

Math.Content.G.SRT.8

27. C: Since there was no figure provided with the problem, a figure should be drawn and labeled as follows:

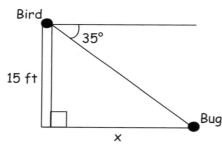

The sight line of the bird looking straight ahead is parallel to the ground, so the 35° angle of depression is congruent to the angle of elevation due to the Alternate Interior Angle Theorem. Therefore, the focus of the problem becomes a right triangle labeled as follows:

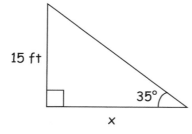

Since the legs opposite and adjacent to the 35° angle are labeled, the equation is set up as $\tan 35° = \frac{15}{x}$. Solving for x, the equation becomes $x = \frac{15}{\tan 35°} = 21.4$ ft. In Answer A, the

- 84 -

equation was incorrectly set up as $\tan 35° = \frac{x}{15}$. In Answer B, the equation was incorrectly set up as $\cos 35° = \frac{15}{x}$. In Answer D, the equation was incorrectly set up as $\sin 35° = \frac{15}{x}$.

Math.Content.G.SRT.9

28. A: The general formula for a triangle is $A = \frac{1}{2} \times base \times height$. In this triangle, the base is length b. For the height of the triangle, draw in an altitude from vertex B perpendicular to side $\overline{AC}$. Then, $\sin C = \frac{height}{a}$. Solving that equation for the height yields $height = a\sin(C)$. Therefore, the formula for the area of a triangle becomes $A = \frac{1}{2} \times b \times a\sin(C)$, which can be rearranged as $A = \frac{1}{2}ab\sin(C)$.

Math.Content.G.SRT.10

29. C: In the figure, since the given angle is located between the two given sides, we need to use the Law of Cosines to solve for x. The Law of Cosines is $c^2 = a^2 + b^2 - 2ab\cos(C)$. If we let $a = 14$, $b = 18$ and $c = x$, then the Law of Cosines becomes $x^2 = 14^2 + 18^2 - 2(14)(18)\cos(53°)$.. This simplifies as $x^2 = 216.69$.. Therefore, $x = 14.7$. Answer A used sine instead of cosine in the formula. Answer B incorrectly used the Pythagorean Theorem with $x^2 + 14^2 = 18^2$, instead of using the Law of Cosines. Answer D also incorrectly used the Pythagorean Theorem with $14^2 + 18^2 = x^2$.

Math.Content.G.SRT.11

30. B: Since the map shows a triangle with a 74° angle, the length of the side opposite the 74° angle, a 56° angle, and it asks for length of the side opposite of the 56° angle (which we will call x), the Law of Sines is needed to find the missing side length. The Law of Sines is $\frac{\sin A}{a} = \frac{\sin B}{b} = \frac{\sin C}{c}$, but to solve this problem we only need $\frac{\sin A}{a} = \frac{\sin B}{b}$. By substitution, that equation becomes $\frac{\sin 74°}{9.3} = \frac{\sin 56°}{x}$. Solving for x, the equation results in $x = \frac{9.3\sin 56°}{\sin 74°} = 8.0$ miles. In Answer A, the equation was incorrectly set up as just $\frac{74}{9.3} = \frac{56}{x}$. In Answer C, the equation was incorrectly set up as $9.3\sin 74° = x\sin 56°$. Answer D is the length of x if the equation was incorrectly set up as $\frac{\cos A}{a} = \frac{\cos B}{b}$.

Math.Content.G.C.1

31. B: In all circles, the formula for the circumference of the circle is $Circumferece = \pi \times Diameter$. If we rearrange that equation, it becomes $\frac{Circumference}{Diameter} = \pi$. Therefore, in any circle, the ratio of the circumference to the diameter is always equal to π. As a result, all circles are similar.

Math.Content.G.C.2

32. C: Since $\overline{AB}$ is tangent to Circle O, then $\overline{AB}$ forms a right angle with radius $\overline{AO}$. ΔAOB is then a right triangle, so the Pythagorean Theorem can be used to find the measure of $\overline{OB}$. Therefore, $(OB)^2 = 8^2 + 15^2 = 64 + 225 =, 289$. After taking the square root of both sides, it becomes $17 = OB$.

Math.Content.G.C.3

33. C: If a quadrilateral is inscribed in a circle, then its opposite angles are supplementary. Therefore, $m\angle ABC + m\angle ADC = 180°$. By substitution, that equation becomes $7x + 4 + 2x +$

14 = 180. The equation simplifies as $9x + 18 = 180$. After subtracting 18 from both sides, the equation becomes $9x = 162$. Divide both sides by 9 to get $x = 18$. Substituting for x in the expression results in 2(18) + 14 = 36 + 14 = 50°. Answer A is the value of x. Answer B is the measure of $\angle ADC$ if $\angle ABC$ and $\angle ADC$ were incorrectly thought to be complementary instead of supplementary. Answer D is the measure if the equation was incorrectly set up as $m\angle ABC + m\angle ADC = 360°$, but 360° is the measure of all four angles.

Math.Content.G.C.4

34. A: For any point outside a circle, there are exactly two lines tangent to the circle passing through that point. Further, the lengths of these line segments from the point to the circle are equal. In this problem, the two segments extending from Q both have a length of 7. The two segments extending from R have a length of 4. The two segments extending from S have a length of 2. The two segments extending from P have a length of 5. Therefore, the perimeter of quadrilateral $PQRS$ can be calculated at 7 + 7 + 4 + 4 + 2 + 2 + 5 + 5 = 36.

Math.Content.G.C.5

35. B: The area of the sector of a circle is calculated using the equation: $\frac{Central\ Angle\ Measure}{360°} \times \pi r^2$, where r is the radius of the circle. Since the central angle measure is 112° and the radius is 9 in, the equation becomes: $\frac{112°}{360°} \times \pi(9\ in)^2 = 79.2$ in². Answer A found the length of the arc intercepted by $\angle RQS$. Answer C is the area of the circle. Answer D used the diameter length instead of the radius in the calculation.

Math.Content.G.GPE.1

36. D: The equation for a circle is $(x - h)^2 + (y - k)^2 = r^2$, where (h, k) is the center of the circle and r is the radius. Since the center of the circle is (–5, 3) and the radius is 4, those values can be substituted into the equation as $\left(x - (-5)\right)^2 + (y - 3)^2 = 4^2$ which simplifies as $(x + 5)^2 + (y - 3)^2 = 16$. Answers A and B did not square the radius. Answers A and C did not subtract the center values from x and y when they were substituted into the equation.

Math.Content.G.GPE.2

37. C: Since the focus is at (2, 3) and the directrix is the line $y = -1$, the vertex of the parabola is halfway between those values. Therefore, the vertex is located at (2, 1). Since the focus is located above the vertex, the parabola opens up. A parabola that opens up has the general equation of $(x - h)^2 = 4p(y - k)$, where (h, k) is the vertex and the absolute value of p is the distance between the focus and the vertex and the distance between the vertex and directrix. In this problem, the focus is (2, 3) and the vertex is (2, 1), so $|p| = |(3 - 1)| = |2| = 2$. Since the focus is above the vertex, the value of p is positive, so $p = 2$. Substituting the values for the vertex and p into the equation, it becomes: $(x - 2)^2 = 4(2)(y - 1)$ and simplifies as $(x - 2)^2 = 8(y - 1)$. Answer A incorrectly set up the equation as $(y - k)^2 = 4p(x - h)$. Answer B incorrectly set up the equation as $(y - k)^2 = 4p(x - h)$ and then incorrectly used the focus for (h, k) and the directrix for p. Answer D correctly used the equation of $(x - h)^2 = 4p(y - k)$, but then incorrectly used the focus for (h, k) and the directrix for p.

Math.Content.G.GPE.3

38. B: Since the foci are located along the line $y = 3$, the major axis of the ellipse is horizontal. This means the general equation for the ellipse is $\frac{(x-h)^2}{a^2} + \frac{(y-k)^2}{b^2} = 1$, where ($h$,

- 86 -

k) is the center of the ellipse, a is half the length of the major axis and b is half the length of the minor axis. Since the center is located between the foci of $(-2, 3)$ and $(4, 3)$, the center of the ellipse is located at $(1, 3)$ and the distance from the center to each focus, c, is 3. The sum of the distances from the foci to a point on the ellipse is equivalent to $2a$. Therefore, $2a = 8$, so $a = 4$ and $a^2 = 16$. To find the value of b^2, we use the equation $b^2 = a^2 - c^2$. Substituting in for that equation, $b^2 = 4^2 - 3^2 = 16 - 9 = 7$. Based on the center $(1, 3)$ and the squares of the axes $a^2 = 16$ and $b^2 = 7$, the equation for the ellipse becomes $\frac{(x-1)^2}{16} + \frac{(y-3)^2}{7} = 1$. Answer A incorrectly set up the equation as $\frac{(x-h)^2}{b^2} + \frac{(y-k)^2}{a^2} = 1$. Answer C incorrectly set up the equation as $\frac{(x-h)^2}{b^2} + \frac{(y-k)^2}{a^2} = 1$ and then incorrectly used $a = 8$, which made $a^2 = 64$ and $b^2 = 64 - 9 = 55$. Answer D incorrectly used $a = 8$, which made $a^2 = 64$ and $b^2 = 64 - 9 = 55$.

Math.Content.G.GPE.4

39. D: A circle centered at $(3, 0)$ that passes through the point $(7, 0)$ has a radius, r, of 4 units, since $r = \sqrt{(7-3)^2 + (0-0)^2} = \sqrt{(4)^2 + (0)^2} = \sqrt{16+0} = \sqrt{16} = 4$. The equation for a circle with a center of $(3, 0)$ and $r = 4$ is $(x - 3)^2 + (y - 0)^2 = 4^2$, which simplifies as $(x - 3)^2 + y^2 = 16$. Substituting in the points above into the circle equation, only Answer D correctly works since $(6 - 3)^2 + \left(\sqrt{7}\right)^2 = (3)^2 + \left(\sqrt{7}\right)^2 = 9 + 7 = 16$. Answer A results if $(0 - 3)^2$ is incorrectly simplified as -9. Answer B results if $(1 - 3)^2$ is incorrectly simplified as -4. Answer C results if $(2 - 3)^2$ is incorrectly simplified as -1.

Math.Content.G.GPE.5

40. D: The slope of the original line is $m = \frac{2}{3}$. Since the new line needs to be perpendicular, the new slope needs to be the negative reciprocal of the original slope. The negative reciprocal of $\frac{2}{3}$ is $-\frac{3}{2}$. The given point is $(6, 2)$, which is equivalent to (x_1, y_1) in the point-slope equation of $y - y_1 = m(x - x_1)$. Substituting in the new slope and given point, the point-slope equation becomes $y - 2 = -\frac{3}{2}(x - 6)$. Distributing on the right side of the equation results in $y - 2 = -\frac{3}{2}x + 9$. Add 2 to both sides of the equation to get the perpendicular line of $y = -\frac{3}{2}x + 11$. Answer A found a parallel line. Answer B took the opposite slope instead of the opposite reciprocal slope. Answer C took the reciprocal slope instead of the opposite reciprocal slope.

Math.Content.G.GPE.6

41. D: If point C is four times farther from A than from B, it means that the ratio of distances from C to A and B is 4:1, respectively. Therefore, the line segment can be broken up into 4 + 1 = 5 equal segments. The total distance between points A and B is 7 – (–3) = 10 units. If we divide 10 by 5, each equal segment is 2 units in length. We can then multiply the ratio by 2 to get the actual distances of C from A and B, 4(2):1(2) = 8:2. So, C is located 8 units from A and 2 units from B. Since A is located at –3, it means that –3 + 8 = 5. Answer A is the location if C is four times farther from B than it is from A. Answer B is just four units from point A. Answer C is just four units from point B.

Math.Content.G.GPE.7

42. D: To find the area of rectangle $ABCD$, first start by plotting the rectangle on a coordinate grid, as shown below.

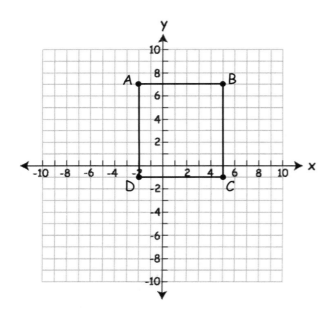

Then, since the sides of the rectangle are parallel to the x and y-axes, find the lengths of *AB* and *BC*. *AB* = 5 –(–2) = 7. *BC* = 7 –(–1) = 8. Therefore, the area of rectangle *ABCD* is (7)(8) = 56 units². Answer A is the area if the length of the sides were incorrectly calculated as *AB* = 5–2 = 3 and *BC* = 7–1 = 6. Answer B is the area if the coordinate values were mixed up and the sides were incorrectly calculated as *AB* = 5–1 = 4 and *BC* = 7–2=5. Answer C is the perimeter of the rectangle.

Math.Content.G.GMD.1

43. B: It is the Informal Limits Argument that uses a regular polygon inscribed in a circle to derive the formula for the area of a circle. When a regular polygon is inscribed in a circle, the polygon can be broken up into many triangles with the vertex at the center of the circle and the base along the edge of the polygon. As the number of sides of the polygon is increased, the number of triangles is also increased. As the number of sides of the polygon gets larger, the combined area of each triangle within that polygon approaches the area of the circle. In Answer A, the Dissection Argument finds the area of a circle by breaking up the circle into wedges and then rearranging those wedges to form a rectangle. In Answer C, the Inscribed Angle Theorem states that the measure of an inscribed angle is half the measure of its intercepted arc. In Answer D, the Pythagorean Theorem states that in a right triangle, the square of the hypotenuse is equal to the sum of the squares of the legs.

Math.Content.G.GMD.2

44. B: Based on Cavalieri's principle, if all corresponding cross sections of two solids have the same area, then those two solids also have the same volume.

Math.Content.G.GMD.3

45. B: The volume of the cylinder is the amount of grain that the farmer will be able to store in the silo. The formula for the volume of a cylinder is $V = \pi r^2 h$, where r is the radius and h is the height. Since the cylinder has a diameter of 8 m, the radius is half of the diameter, or 4 m. The height is 24 m. Therefore, by substitution, $V = \pi r^2 h$ becomes $V = \pi (4\ m)^2 (24\ m)=$ 1,206.4 m³. Answer A used the volume formula for a cone. Answer C used the volume formula for a cone and the diameter of the cylinder. Answer D used the diameter instead of the radius in the volume formula.

Math.Content.G.GMD.3

46. A: The volume of the sugar cone is the amount of ice cream needed to completely fill in the sugar cone with ice cream. The formula for the volume of a cone is $V = \frac{1}{3}\pi r^2 h$, where r is the radius and h is the height of the cone. Since the cone has a diameter of 5 cm, the radius is half of the diameter, or 2.5 cm. The height of the cone is 12.5 cm. Therefore, by substitution, $V = \frac{1}{3}\pi r^2 h$ becomes $V = \frac{1}{3}\pi(2.5\ cm)^2(12.5\ cm) = 81.8$ cm³. Answer B forgot to multiply by $\frac{1}{3}$. Answer C used the diameter instead of the radius in the formula. Answer D forgot to multiply by $\frac{1}{3}$ and used the diameter instead of the radius.

Math.Content.G.GMD.4

47. A: When a horizontal cross-section is taken of the triangular prism shown, the cross-section is parallel to the rectangular side along the ground. Therefore, the resulting two-dimensional shape is a rectangle. Answer C would be the result if a vertical cross-section was taken parallel to the triangle bases.

Math.Content.G.MG.1

48. C: The formula for the volume of a pyramid is $V = \frac{1}{3}BH$, where B is the area of the base and H is the height of the pyramid. Since the base is a square with a length of 756 ft on each side, the area of the base is A = s^2 = (756 ft)² = 571,536 ft². Therefore, with a base of 571,536 ft² and a height of 481 ft, the volume of the Great Pyramid of Khufu is $V = \frac{1}{3}(571,536\ ft^2)(481\ ft)$= 9.16 × 10⁷ ft³. Answer A just used the length of one side of the square for the base instead of the area of the base. Answer B used the perimeter of the base instead of the area. Answer D incorrectly used the formula $V = BH$.

Math.Content.G.MG.2

49. B: Population density is calculated by taking the population of a city and dividing that value by the square miles of land in the city. For Minneapolis, the population density is calculated as $\frac{382,578\ persons}{54.9\ square\ miles}$ = 6,968.6 persons/square mile. Answer A incorrectly calculated the population density by dividing 382,578 by 54.9². Answer C incorrectly multiplied the population by the land area. Answer D incorrectly multiplied the population by the 54.9².

Math.Content.G.MG.3

50. D: The cost for filling the sand box with sand is calculated by multiplying the cost/bag of sand by the number of bags needed. To determine the number of bags needed, first find the volume of the sand box: 6 ft× 4 ft× 1 ft = 24 cubic feet. Next, since each bag of sand contains 0.5 cubic feet of sand, the number of bags needed is $\frac{24\ cubic\ feet}{0.5\ cubic\ feet/bag}$ = 48 bags. Finally, since the cost/bag is $3.75, the cost for filling the sand box is $3.75/bag × 48 bags = $180. In Answer A, 24 is just the volume of the sand box. Answer B is the value if the number of bags of sand was incorrectly calculated by multiplying 24 × 0.5 instead of dividing 24÷0.5. Answer C is the value if the number of bags of sand was incorrectly thought to be the same as the volume of the box.

Practice Test #2

Practice Questions

1. "The set of all points that are a fixed distance from a given point" is the definition for which of the following terms?

Ⓐ Angle

Ⓑ Circle

Ⓒ Line Segment

Ⓓ Ray

2. Determine which of the following transformations preserves distance and angle.

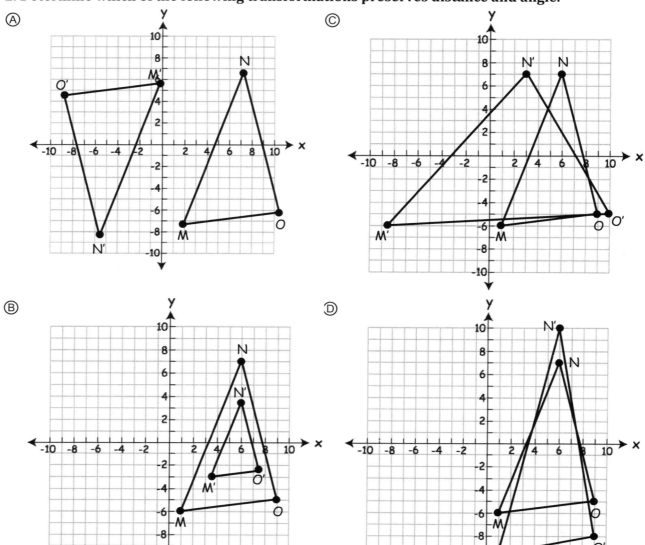

3. Based on the figure below, describe how rectangle *ABCD* can be carried onto its image *A′B′C′D′*.

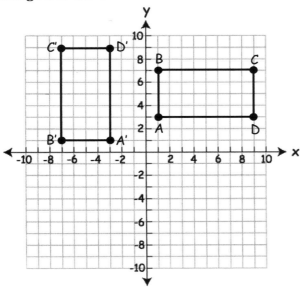

Ⓐ Reflection across the x-axis

Ⓑ Reflection across the y-axis

Ⓒ Rotation 90° clockwise about the origin

Ⓓ Rotation 90° counterclockwise about the origin

4. Examine the figure.

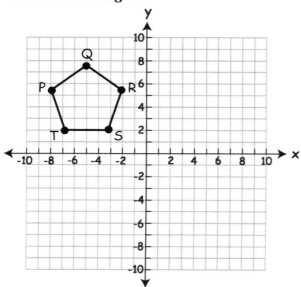

Identify the image $P'Q'R'S'T'$ that results if $PQRST$ is reflected across the line $y = x$.

Ⓐ

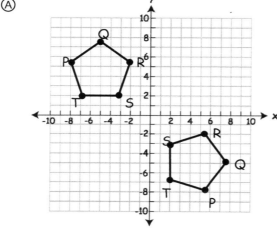

Ⓒ

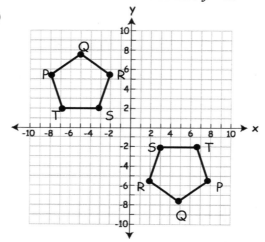

Ⓑ

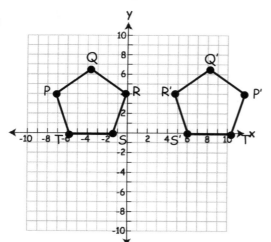

Ⓓ

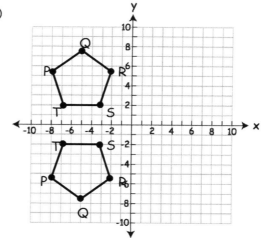

5. If $\overleftrightarrow{AB}$ was rotated 180° about the origin to form its image $\overleftrightarrow{A'B'}$, what type of lines would $\overleftrightarrow{AB}$ and $\overleftrightarrow{A'B'}$ create?

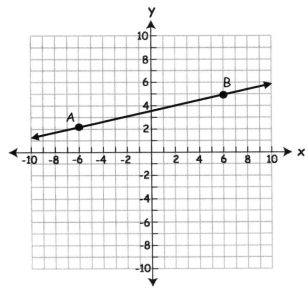

    Ⓐ Intersecting Lines

    Ⓑ Parallel Lines

    Ⓒ Perpendicular Lines

    Ⓓ Skew Lines

6. Which of the following terms is defined as "A transformation in which every point of a figure is moved the same distance and in the same direction to create the image"?

    Ⓐ Translation

    Ⓑ Rotation

    Ⓒ Reflection

    Ⓓ Dilation

7. Examine the figure below.

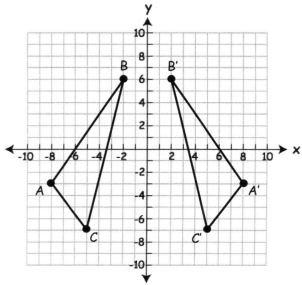

Which of the following transformations occurred to get from ΔABC to ΔA′B′C′?

Ⓐ Dilation

Ⓑ Reflection

Ⓒ Rotation

Ⓓ Translation

8. Examine the figure below.

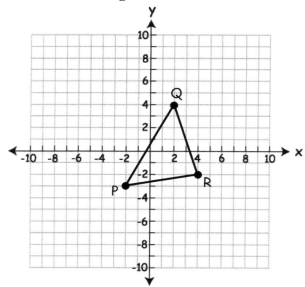

If ΔPQR were translated by the rule $(x, y) \rightarrow (x - 4, y + 2)$, what would be the resulting image ΔP′Q′R′?

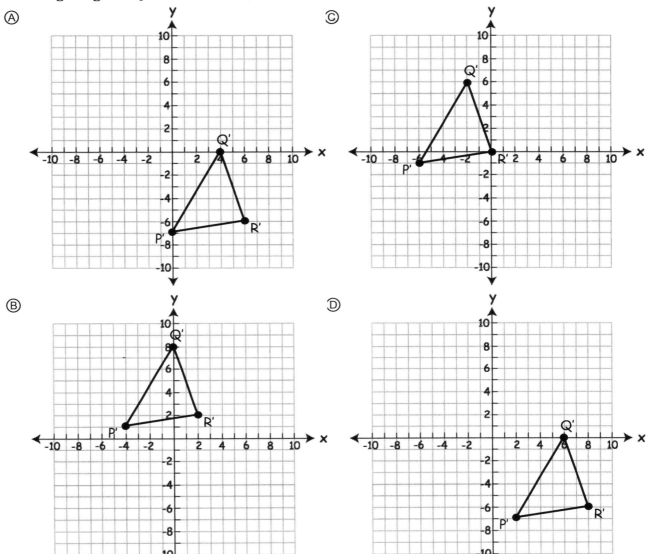

9. Based on the triangle markings, which pair of triangles is congruent?

Ⓐ

Ⓑ

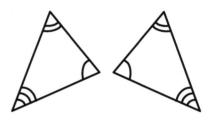

Ⓒ

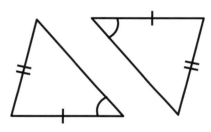

Ⓓ

 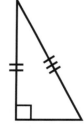

10. Examine the figure below.

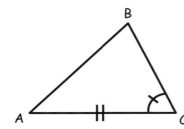 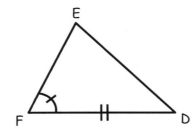

In order to prove that $\triangle ABC \cong \triangle DEF$ by SAS triangle congruence, which of the following corresponding parts of the triangle must also be congruent?

Ⓐ $\overline{AB} \cong \overline{DE}$

Ⓑ $\overline{AB} \cong \overline{EF}$

Ⓒ $\overline{BC} \cong \overline{DE}$

Ⓓ $\overline{BC} \cong \overline{EF}$

11. Which triangle congruence can be used to prove that $\triangle ABC \cong \triangle DBC$?

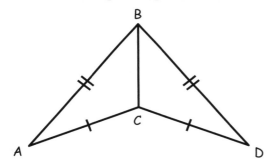

Ⓐ AAS

Ⓑ ASA

Ⓒ SAS

Ⓓ SSS

- 99 -

12. Examine the figure below.

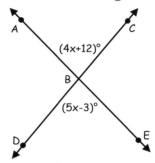

What is the measure of ∠ABC?

Ⓐ 15°

Ⓑ 48°

Ⓒ 72°

Ⓓ 88°

13. Lines *p* and *q* are parallel in the figure below. If $m\angle 3 = 8x + 24$ and $m\angle 7 = 10x - 6$, what is the measure of ∠4?

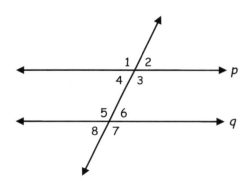

Ⓐ 15°

Ⓑ 36°

Ⓒ 86°

Ⓓ 144°

14. Find the measure of $\overline{BD}$ in the figure below.

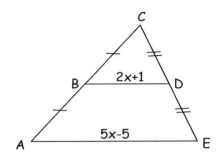

Ⓐ 2

Ⓑ 5

Ⓒ 7

Ⓓ 15

15. *JKLM* is a parallelogram. If *JL* = 13*x* − 11 and *JN* = 4*x* + 7, what is the length of $\overline{JN}$.?

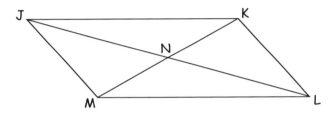

Ⓐ 2

Ⓑ 5

Ⓒ 15

Ⓓ 27

16. The statement "Without changing the compass width, place the compass on the new point, which is not on the segment, and then draw an arc in the area where the other endpoint will be located" is a necessary step in which of the following compass and straightedge constructions?

Ⓐ Bisecting a line segment

Ⓑ Copying a line segment

Ⓒ Drawing parallel lines

Ⓓ Drawing perpendicular lines

17. Which of the following steps is needed to construct a square inscribed in a circle?

Ⓐ Without changing the compass width, place the compass on the new point, which is not on the segment, and then draw an arc in the area where the other endpoint will be located.

Ⓑ Using a straightedge, draw a line from the angle vertex to the point where the two arcs intersect on the interior of the angle.

Ⓒ Draw in the diameter of the circle and label the endpoints as B and C. Set your compass wider than it was to draw the circle and draw another circle, using B as the center.

Ⓓ With the compass set to the same width as the radius, center the compass at a point on the circle and then draw an arc across the circle. Mark the point of intersection across the circle, then center the compass at the intersection point and repeat the steps to draw arcs around the circle.

18. If parallelogram $WXYZ$, shown below, is dilated by a scale factor of 3 to create image $W'X'Y'Z'$, what is the relationship between $\overleftrightarrow{WZ}$ and $\overleftrightarrow{W'Z'}$?

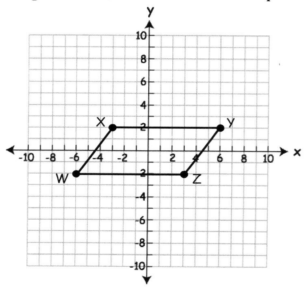

Ⓐ $\overleftrightarrow{WZ}$ and $\overleftrightarrow{W'Z'}$ are parallel.

Ⓑ $\overleftrightarrow{WZ}$ and $\overleftrightarrow{W'Z'}$ are perpendicular.

Ⓒ $\overleftrightarrow{W'Z'}$ has a slope 3 times that of $\overleftrightarrow{WZ}$.

Ⓓ $\overleftrightarrow{W'Z'}$ has a slope $\frac{1}{3}$ times that of $\overleftrightarrow{WZ}$.

19. In the figure below, ΔJKL is dilated to the image ΔJ′K′L′.

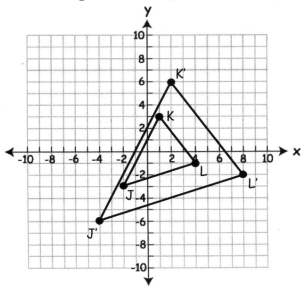

What is the scale factor of the dilation?

Ⓐ $\frac{1}{3}$

Ⓑ $\frac{1}{2}$

Ⓒ 2

Ⓓ 3

20. Examine the triangles below:

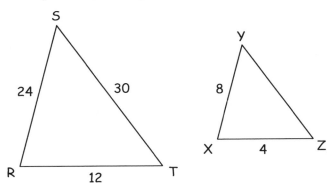

In order for ΔRST to be similar to ΔXYZ, what must be the length of $\overline{YZ}$?

Ⓐ 10

Ⓑ 14

Ⓒ 15

Ⓓ 22

21. Determine which of the following triangles can be proved similar by the AA Similarity Theorem.

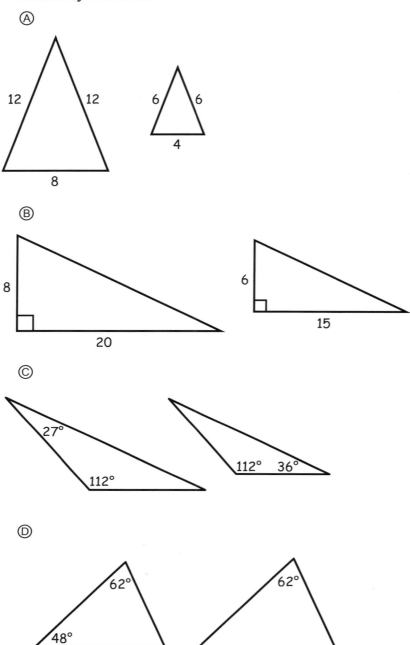

22. In $\triangle ABC$, $\overline{DE} \parallel \overline{AC}$.

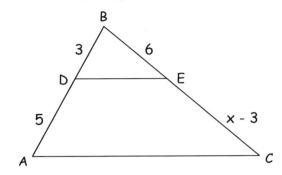

Solve for *x*.

   Ⓐ 8

   Ⓑ 10

   Ⓒ 11

   Ⓓ 13

23. Examine the figure below, in which $\triangle JKL \sim \triangle RST$.

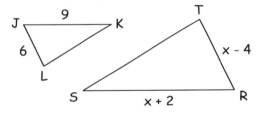

What is the length of $\overline{RS}$?

   Ⓐ 10

   Ⓑ 12

   Ⓒ 16

   Ⓓ 18

24. The ratio $\dfrac{opposite\ leg}{adjacent\ leg}$ represents which trigonometric function?

   Ⓐ Sine

   Ⓑ Cosine

   Ⓒ Tangent

   Ⓓ Secant

25. Which of the following pairs of values are equivalent?

Ⓐ sin 17°, cos 73°

Ⓑ sin 58°, cos 58°

Ⓒ sin 64°, sin 26°

Ⓓ sin 145°, sin 35°

26. A building is installing a new ramp at their front entrance.

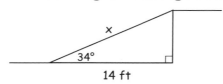

Based on the figure above, what is the length of the ramp, shown by *x*?

Ⓐ 11.6 ft

Ⓑ 16.9 ft

Ⓒ 20.8 ft

Ⓓ 25.0 ft

27. Two hikers start at a ranger station and leave at the same time. One hiker heads due west at 3 miles/hour. The other hiker heads due north at 4 miles/hour. How far apart are the hikers after 2 hours of hiking?

Ⓐ 5 miles

Ⓑ 7 miles

Ⓒ 10 miles

Ⓓ 14 miles

28. The height, _h_, of the triangle below can also be represented by which of the following expressions?

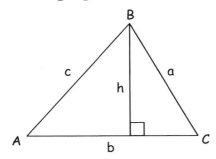

Ⓐ $h = a\cos(C)$

Ⓑ $h = a\sin(C)$

Ⓒ $h = b\cos(C)$

Ⓓ $h = b\sin(C)$

29. Examine the following triangle:

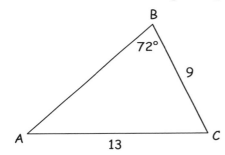

What is the approximate measure of ∠A?

Ⓐ 41°

Ⓑ 54°

Ⓒ 67°

Ⓓ 78°

30. While recording the measurements for a plot of land, a surveyor notices a small pond on the property. The surveyor is not able to measure the largest width across the pond directly, but he is able to make the following measurements:

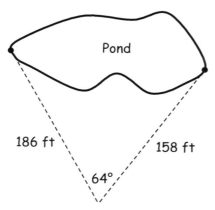

What is the largest distance across the pond?

Ⓐ 82.1 ft

Ⓑ 98.1 ft

Ⓒ 183.8 ft

Ⓓ 244.0 ft

31. Which of the following statements about circles is true?

Ⓐ All circles are similar.

Ⓑ All circles are congruent.

Ⓒ All circles have the same area.

Ⓓ All circles have the same circumference.

32. Based on the figure below, solve for *x*.

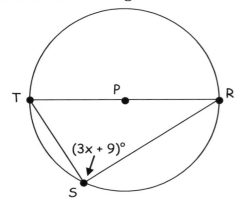

Ⓐ x = 12

Ⓑ x = 17

Ⓒ x = 27

Ⓓ x = 57

33. In Circle O, find the measure of ∠RTS.

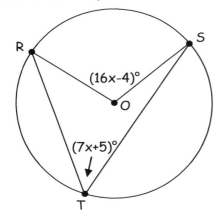

Ⓐ 12°

Ⓑ 26°

Ⓒ 54°

Ⓓ 108°

34. $\overline{AC}$ and $\overline{BC}$ are tangent to the circle. What is the length of $\overline{AC}$?

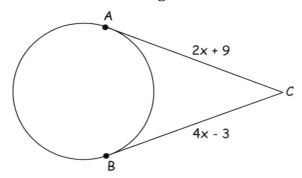

(A) 6

(B) 13

(C) 15

(D) 21

35. Find the length of the arc intercepted by $\angle AOB$.

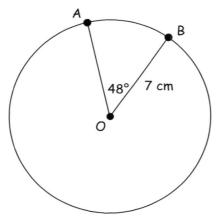

(A) 5.9 cm

(B) 11.7 cm

(C) 20.5 cm

(D) 44.0 cm

36. Find the center and radius of a circle defined by the equation: $x^2 + 2x + y^2 - 8y + 8 = 0.$

    Ⓐ $(-1, 4), r = 3$

    Ⓑ $(1, -4), r = 9$

    Ⓒ $(-2, 8), r = 3$

    Ⓓ $(2, -8), r = 9$

37. Find the equation for a parabola with focus (3, –3) and directrix $x = -5.$

    Ⓐ $(x + 1)^2 = -20(y + 3)$

    Ⓑ $(x + 1)^2 = 16(y + 3)$

    Ⓒ $(y + 3)^2 = -20(x - 3)$

    Ⓓ $(y + 3)^2 = 16(x + 1)$

38. Given a hyperbola with foci (5, –4) and (5, 8) and a difference of the distances from the foci to a point on the hyperbola of 10, what is the equation of the hyperbola?

    Ⓐ $\frac{(x-5)^2}{25} + \frac{(y-2)^2}{11} = 1$

    Ⓑ $\frac{(x-5)^2}{25} - \frac{(y-2)^2}{11} = 1$

    Ⓒ $\frac{(y-2)^2}{25} + \frac{(x-5)^2}{11} = 1$

    Ⓓ $\frac{(y-2)^2}{25} - \frac{(x-5)^2}{11} = 1$

39. A quadrilateral has the following coordinates $P(-1, 4)$, $Q(5, 2)$, $R(4, -1)$ **and** $T(-2, 1)$. **Quadrilateral** *PQRS* **can be best defined as which of the following shapes?**

    Ⓐ Trapezoid

    Ⓑ Square

    Ⓒ Rectangle

    Ⓓ Parallelogram

40. Which of the following equations represents a line parallel to the line $y = -\frac{1}{2}x + 3$ **and passes through the point (–4, –2).**

    Ⓐ $x + 2y = 8$

    Ⓑ $x + 2y = -8$

    Ⓒ $2x - y = 6$

    Ⓓ $2x - y = -6$

41. Examine the number line below.

Identify the location of a point *T* on the number line between *R* and *S* such that *T* is twice as far from *S* as it is from *R*.

(A) 4

(B) 6

(C) 8

(D) 10

42. Find the perimeter of △*ABC* in the figure below.

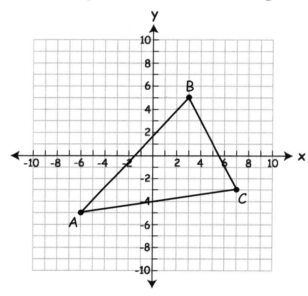

(A) 11.69 units

(B) 21.26 units

(C) 24.14 units

(D) 35.54 units

43. One method for calculating the area of a circle is to dissect it into a number of wedges. The circle below has a radius *r* and has been evenly dissected into 16 wedges.

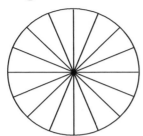

If the wedges are rearranged alternately to create a shape resembling a rectangle, as shown below, what is the approximate length of the rectangle?

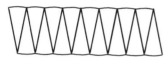

    Ⓐ π

    Ⓑ πr

    Ⓒ r

    Ⓓ πr^2

44. While comparing two cones, a student notices that all corresponding cross sections of the cones have the same area. As a result, the student determines that the two cones also have the same volume. The student just discovered which of the following?

    Ⓐ Euclid's Principle

    Ⓑ Cavalieri's Principle

    Ⓒ Dissection Argument

    Ⓓ Informal Limit Argument

45. At a sand sculpture festival, one group plans to build a giant sand pyramid on the beach. If the base of the pyramid is to be a square with sides of 10 ft and the pyramid is to be 12 ft tall, how much sand will be needed to build the pyramid?

    Ⓐ 260 ft3

    Ⓑ 400 ft3

    Ⓒ 520 ft3

    Ⓓ 1,200 ft3

46. Kelsey is having a pool party and brought beach balls for the guests to use in the pool. When inflated, each beach ball is 12 inches in diameter. How much air is needed to inflate each beach ball?

    (A) 904.8 in³

    (B) 2,714.3 in³

    (C) 7,238.2 in³

    (D) 21,714.7 in³

47. If the following shape was rotated about the identified axis, what 3-D object will be generated?

Rotation
Axis

    (A) Cube

    (B) Cylinder

    (C) Rectangular Prism

    (D) Sphere

48. The shape of Earth can be closely represented by a sphere with a radius of 6,378.1 km. What is the approximate surface area of Earth?

    (A) 1.70 × 108 km²

    (B) 5.11 × 108 km²

    (C) 1.09 × 1012 km²

    (D) 3.26 × 10¹² km²

49. A local craft store specializes in selling marbles. To display their most popular sized marble, the store created a 3 ft× 2 ft × 6 in glass box and completely filled the box with 5,184 marbles. What is the density of marbles per cubic foot in the glass box?

Ⓐ 144 marbles/cubic foot

Ⓑ 864 marbles/cubic foot

Ⓒ 1,728 marbles/cubic foot

Ⓓ 15,522 marbles/cubic foot

50. A city has decided to build a fountain in the center of its new park. A 30 ft × 30 ft plot of land will be used for the fountain area. The fountain, which will be circular with a 16 ft diameter, will be centered within that plot of land and the remaining area surrounding the fountain will be covered by a cement walkway. How much land will be covered by the walkway?

Ⓐ 95.8 ft²

Ⓑ 201.1 ft²

Ⓒ 698.9 ft²

Ⓓ 900.0 ft²

Answers and Explanations

Math.Content.G.CO.1

1. B: A circle is defined as the set of all points that are a fixed distance from a given point. In Answer A, an angle is defined as two rays that share a common endpoint. In Answer C, a line segment is defined as all points between and including two given points. In Answer D, a ray is a part of a line starting at a particular point and extending indefinitely in one direction.

Math.Content.G.CO.2

2. A: In Answer A, $\Delta M'N'O'$ is a 180° rotation about the origin of ΔMNO. Therefore, the rotation in Answer A is the transformation that preserves the distance and angle of the original image. Answer B is a dilation of the original image, so it does not preserve distance. Answer C is a horizontal stretch of the original image, so it does not preserve distance or angle. Answer D is a vertical stretching, so it also does not preserve distance or angle.

Math.Content.G.CO.3

3. D: As rectangle $ABCD$ is moved from Quadrant I into Quadrant II, it is rotated in a counterclockwise manner. Therefore, rectangle $ABCD$ can be carried onto its image $A'B'C'D'$ by a 90° counterclockwise rotation about the origin.

Math.Content.G.CO.3

4. A: If a figure is reflected across the line $y = x$, the coordinates of the original figure change from (x, y) to (y, x). In Answer A, the coordinates of image $P'Q'R'S'T'$ are in the order of (y, x) compared to the (x, y) coordinates of $PQRST$, so Answer A shows a reflection across the line $y = x$. Answer B is a reflection across the y-axis. Answer C is a 180° rotation about the origin. Answer D is a reflection across the x-axis.

Math.Content.G.CO.4

5. B: In $\overleftrightarrow{AB}$, A is located at (−6, 2) and B is located at (6, 5). The slope of $\overleftrightarrow{AB} = \frac{5-2}{6-(-6)} = \frac{3}{12} = \frac{1}{4}$. When $\overleftrightarrow{AB}$ is rotated 180° about the origin, the coordinate point for A' becomes (6, −2) and the coordinate point for B' becomes (−6,−5). The slope of $\overleftrightarrow{A'B'} = \frac{-5-(-2)}{-6-6} = \frac{-3}{-12} = \frac{1}{4}$. Since $\overleftrightarrow{AB}$ and $\overleftrightarrow{A'B'}$ have the same slope, the lines are parallel.

Math.Content.G.CO.4

6. A: A translation moves every point of a figure the same distance and in the same direction to create an image. In Answer B, a rotation turns a figure around a central point. In Answer C, a reflection reflects a figure across a given line to create a mirror image. In Answer D, a dilation changes the size of a figure while still maintaining its shape.

Math.Content.G.CO.5

7. B: In the figure, ΔABC was reflected across the y-axis to get $\Delta A'B'C'$. Therefore, the transformation that occurred was a reflection. A dilation would have changed the size of ΔABC while maintaining the shape. A rotation would have rotated ΔABC about a central point. A translation would have moved each point in ΔABC by the same distance and in the same direction.

Math.Content.G.CO.6

8. C: The translation rule $(x, y) \rightarrow (x - 4, y + 2)$ means that 4 is subtracted from each x-coordinate (or each x-coordinate moves 4 units to the left) and 2 is added to each y-coordinate (or each y-coordinate moves up 2 units). $\Delta P'Q'R'$ in Answer C has each x-coordinate move 4 units left and each y-coordinate move 2 units up. Answer D incorrectly took $x - 4$ to mean move 4 units to the right and took $y + 2$ to mean move 2 units down, as would be the case in equations such as $y = a(x - h)^2 + k$. Answer B had the x and y directions reversed on the coordinate grid. Answer A reversed the x and y directions and moved in the opposite directions, as in Answer B.

Math.Content.G.CO.7

9. A: Two triangles are congruent if and only if corresponding pairs of sides and corresponding pairs of angles are congruent. The triangles in Answer A have all three pairs of corresponding sides and all three pairs of corresponding angles marked congruent. In Answer B, the triangles only show three pairs of congruent sides, so there is not enough information to show that the triangles are congruent. Answer C has two pair of corresponding congruent sides and a pair of non-included angles that are congruent which means there is not enough information to show that those triangles are congruent. Answer D has two right triangles with congruent right angles and congruent hypotenuses, but the corresponding legs are not marked as congruent, so there is not enough information to show that those triangles are congruent.

Math.Content.G.CO.8

10. D: For two triangles to be proved congruent by SAS, the triangles need two pairs of corresponding congruent sides and the angle between them also needs to be congruent. In order to include the given congruent angles, the needed pair of congruent sides must be $\overline{BC} \cong \overline{EF}$.

Math.Content.G.CO.8

11. D: In the figure, it shows that $\overline{AC} \cong \overline{DC}$ and $\overline{AB} \cong \overline{DB}$. Although there is no congruent marking on side BC, since the two triangles share that side, it must be that $\overline{BC} \cong \overline{BC}$ by the reflexive property. Therefore, since all three pairs of corresponding sides are congruent, then $\Delta ABC \cong \Delta DBC$ by the SSS triangle congruence.

Math.Content.G.CO.9

12. C: In order to find the measure of $\angle ABC$, we first need to solve for x. In the figure, the angles are vertical angles. According to the Vertical Angle Theorem, vertical angles are congruent. Therefore, to solve for x, we set up an equation as $4x+12 = 5x-3$. After subtracting $4x$ from both sides and adding 3 to both sides, the equation becomes $15 = x$. Next, substitute the value of x into the expression for the measure of $\angle ABC$: $4(15)+12 = 60+12 = 72°$. Answer A is just the value of x. Answer B is the measure of $\angle ABC$ if the angles were incorrectly treated as complementary. Answer D is the measure of $\angle ABC$ if the angles were incorrectly treated as supplementary.

Math.Content.G.CO.9

13. B: The Corresponding Angles Theorem states that if two parallel lines are cut by a transversal, then the pairs of corresponding angles are congruent. Since $\angle 3$ and $\angle 7$ are corresponding and lines p and q are parallel, then $\angle 3 \cong \angle 7$, which means that $m\angle 3 = m\angle 7$.

By substitution, that equation becomes $8x + 24 = 10x - 6$. After subtracting $8x$ from both sides and adding 6 to both sides, the equation simplifies as $30 = 2x$. Divide both sides by 2 to get $15 = x$. Substituting for the value of x, $m\angle 3 = 8(15) + 24 = 120 + 24 = 144°$. Based on the figure, it is seen that $\angle 3$ and $\angle 4$ are supplementary, so $m\angle 3 + m\angle 4 = 180°$. After substituting for the measure of $\angle 3$, the equation becomes $144° + m\angle 4 = 180°$. Subtract 144 from both sides to get $m\angle 4 = 36°$. Answer A is the value of x. Answer C is the $m\angle 4$ if $\angle 3$ and $\angle 7$ were incorrectly set up as supplementary angles. Answer D is the measure of $\angle 3$.

Math.Content.G.CO.10

14. D: According to the Mid-Segment Theorem, the segment joining the midpoints of the two sides of a triangle is half the length of the third side. Therefore, $AE = 2(BD)$, so by substitution, $5x - 5 = 2(2x + 1)$. This equation can be simplified as $5x - 5 = 4x + 2$. After subtracting $4x$ from both sides and adding 5 to both sides, the equation becomes $x = 7$. To find the measure of $\overline{BD}$, substitute for x to get $2(7) + 1 = 14 + 1 = 15$. Answer A is the value of x if the equation was incorrectly set up as $AE = BD$. Answer B is the measure of $\overline{BD}$ if the equation was incorrectly set up as $AE = BD$. Answer C is just the value of x, but the question asks for the measure of $\overline{BD}$.

Math.Content.G.CO.11

15. D: Based on the figure, we can see that $JN + NL = JL$. One of the theorems about parallelograms states that the diagonals of a parallelogram bisect each other. Therefore, according to the figure, $JN = NL$, which means that the equation $JN + NL = JL$ can be rewritten as $JN + JN = JL$. Substituting the expressions for JL and JN, the equation becomes $4x + 7 + 4x + 7 = 13x - 11$. Simplifying the left side of the equation results in $8x + 14 = 13x - 11$. After subtracting $8x$ from both sides and adding 11 to both sides, the equation becomes $25 = 5x$. Divide both sides of the equation by 5 to get $5 = x$. Then, substitute that value for x into the expression for JN: $4(5) + 7 = 20 + 7 = 27$. Answer B is just the value of x. Answer A is the value for x if the equation was incorrectly set up as just $4x + 7 = 13x - 11$. Answer C is the length of $\overline{JN}$ if the equation was incorrectly set up as $4x + 7 = 13x - 11$.

Math.Content.G.CO.12

16. B: "Without changing the compass width, place the compass on the new point, which is not on the segment, and then draw an arc in the area where the other endpoint will be located" is a necessary step when copying a line segment.

Math.Content.G.CO.13

17. C: In order to inscribe a square in a circle, it is necessary to use the endpoints of the diameter as circle centers and draw two intersecting circles. Therefore, Answer C is the step needed to construct a square inscribed in a circle. Answer A is a step in copying a line segment. Answer B is a step in bisecting an angle. Answer D is a step in inscribing an equilateral triangle or a hexagon in a circle.

Math.Content.G.SRT.1a

18. A: The coordinates of points W and Z are $W(-6, -2)$ and $Z(3, -2)$, which creates a slope for $\overleftrightarrow{WZ} = \frac{-2-(-2)}{3-(-6)} = \frac{0}{9} = 0$. After the dilation by a scale factor of 3, the coordinates of points W' and Z' are $W'(-18, -6)$ and $Z'(9, -6)$, which creates a slope for $\overleftrightarrow{W'Z'} = \frac{-6-(-6)}{9-(-18)} = \frac{0}{27}$. Since $\overleftrightarrow{WZ}$ and $\overleftrightarrow{W'Z'}$ both have a slope of 0, the lines are parallel to each other.

Math.Content.G.SRT.1b

19. C: To determine the scale factor of the dilation, compare the coordinates of $\Delta J'K'L'$ to the coordinates of ΔJKL. J is at $(-2, -3)$ and J' is at $(-4, -6)$, which means that the coordinates of J were multiplied by a scale factor of 2 to get the coordinates of J'. K is at $(1, 3)$ and K' is at $(2, 6)$. L is at $(4, -1)$ and L' is at $(8, -2)$. As can be seen, the coordinates of K and L were also multiplied by a scale factor of 2 to get to the coordinates of K' and L'. Answer B is the scale factor going from $\Delta J'K'L'$ to ΔJKL. Answer D results if 3 was incorrectly added or subtracted from the y-coordinates in points K and L to get K' and L'. Answer A is the reciprocal of answer D.

Math.Content.G.SRT.2

20. A: If two triangles are similar, then all pairs of corresponding sides are proportional. In order for ΔRST to be similar to ΔXYZ, we need $\frac{RS}{XY} = \frac{RT}{XZ} = \frac{ST}{YZ}$. Substituting in for those values becomes $\frac{24}{8} = \frac{12}{4} = \frac{30}{YZ}$. Simplifying the fractions results in $\frac{3}{1} = \frac{3}{1} = \frac{30}{YZ}$. Therefore, in order for the triangles to be similar, we need $\frac{3}{1} = \frac{30}{YZ}$. After cross-multiplying the terms, it becomes $3(YZ) = 30(1)$, $3(YZ) = 30$. Divide both sides by 3 to get $YZ = 10$. Answer B saw that 30 was 6 more than 24 and then incorrectly added 6 to 8 to get 14. Answer C incorrectly set up the scale factor as $\frac{24}{8} = \frac{2}{1}$ and set $\frac{2}{1} = \frac{30}{YZ}$ to get $YZ = 15$. Answer D saw that 30 was 18 more than 12 and then incorrectly added 18 to 4 to get 22.

Math.Content.G.SRT.3

21. D: The triangles in Answer D do not have any sides listed and the two corresponding angles that are listed are congruent. Therefore, the triangles in Answer D can be proved similar using the AA Similarity Theorem. In Answer A, the triangles are similar by the SSS Similarity Theorem since all corresponding sides are proportional. In Answer B, the triangles are similar by the SAS similarity theorem since the two pairs of corresponding sides are proportional and the angles between the sides are congruent. In Answer C, the triangles are not similar since the first triangle has angles of 112°, 27° and then 41°, while the second triangle has angles of 112°, 36° and 32°.

Math.Content.G.SRT.4

22. D: One theorem about triangles states that a line parallel to one side of a triangle divides the other two sides proportionally. Since $\overline{DE} \parallel \overline{AC}$, it means that $\frac{BD}{DA} = \frac{BE}{EC}$. Substituting in for those values results in $\frac{3}{5} = \frac{6}{x-3}$. After cross-multiplying, the equation becomes $3(x-3) = (6)(5)$, which simplifies as $3x - 9 = 30$. After adding 9 to both sides, the equation is now $3x = 39$. Divide both sides by 3 to get $x = 13$. Answer A incorrectly results if it is believed that $x - 3$ is equivalent to the 5 on the other side of the triangle. Answer B is the length of $\overline{EC}$, but not the value of x. Answer C incorrectly results if it is believed that since 5 is two more than 3, that $x - 3$ should be two more than 6, such that $x - 3 = 8$.

Math.Content.G.SRT.5

23. D: Since $\Delta JKL \sim \Delta RST$, it means that the sides are proportional. Therefore, $\frac{JL}{RT} = \frac{JK}{RS}$. Substituting for those segments leads to the proportion $\frac{6}{x-4} = \frac{9}{x+2}$. Cross-multiplying results in $6(x+2) = 9(x-4)$. After distributing, the equation becomes $6x + 12 = 9x - 36$. Subtract $6x$ from both sides and add 36 to both sides to get $48 = 3x$. Divide both sides by 3 to get $16 = x$. Substituting 16 in for x, the length of $\overline{RS} = 16 + 2 = 18$. In Answer A, $6x + 12 = 9x - 36$ was

- 119 -

incorrectly simplified with 36 − 12 instead of 12 + 36 to get 24 = 3x and 8 = x, which led to the length of 8 + 2 = 10. Answer B is the length of $\overline{RT}$ instead of $\overline{RS}$. Answer C is the value of x instead of the length of $\overline{RS}$.

Math.Content.G.SRT.6

24. C: The ratio $\frac{opposite\ leg}{adjacent\ leg}$ represents the tangent function. In Answer A, sine is $\frac{opposite\ leg}{hypotenuse}$. In Answer B, cosine is $\frac{adjacent\ leg}{hypotenuse}$. In Answer D, secant is $\frac{hypotenuse}{adjacent\ leg}$.

Math.Content.G.SRT.7

25. A: The sine of one angle is equivalent to the cosine of the complementary angle, that is $\sin a = \cos(90 - a)$. Therefore, in Answer A, 17° and 73° are complementary angles, so sin 17° = cos 73°. Answer B is the cosine of the same angle instead of the complementary angle value. Answer C is the complementary angle, but it is in terms of sine instead of cosine. Answer D uses supplementary angles instead of complementary angles, and they are both sine instead of one being cosine.

Math.Content.G.SRT.8

26. B: Based on the location of the 34°, the 14 ft section is the adjacent leg and the ramp length is the hypotenuse of the right triangle. Therefore, in order to solve for x, it needs to be set up as $\cos 34° = \frac{adjacent\ leg}{hypotenuse}$ or $\cos 34° = \frac{14}{x}$. The value of x is found using the calculation $x = \frac{14}{\cos 34°} = 16.9$ ft. Answer A incorrectly set up the equation as $\cos 34° = \frac{x}{14}$. Answer C incorrectly used $\tan 34° = \frac{14}{x}$. Answer D incorrectly used $\sin 34° = \frac{14}{x}$.

Math.Content.G.SRT.8

27. C: Hiking due west at 3 miles/hour, the first hiker will have gone 6 miles after 2 hours. Hiking due north at 4 miles/hour, the second hiker will have gone 8 miles after 2 hours. Since one hiker headed west and the other headed north, their distance from each other can be drawn as:

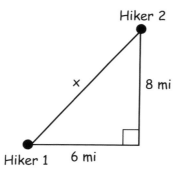

Since the distance between the two hikers is the hypotenuse of a right triangle and we know the lengths of the two legs of the right triangle, the Pythagorean Theorem $(a^2 + b^2 = c^2)$ is used to find the value of x. Therefore, $6^2 + 8^2 = x^2$, $36 + 64 = x^2$, $100 = x^2$, $10 = x$. Answer A is the distance between the hikers after only 1 hour of hiking. Answer B incorrectly added the distances hiked after 1 hour. Answer D incorrectly added the distances hiked after 2 hours.

Math.Content.G.SRT.9

28. B: In relation to $\angle C$, the height, h, is the opposite leg of the right triangle and side a is the hypotenuse of the right triangle. Therefore, $\sin(C) = \frac{opposite\ leg}{hypotenuse}$, which can be rewritten as $\sin(C) = \frac{h}{a}$. Solving for h results in $h = a \sin(C)$.

Math.Content.G.SRT.10

29. A: Since the figure shows the measure of $\angle B$, the length of the side opposite of $\angle B$, the length of the side opposite of $\angle A$, and it asks for the measure of $\angle A$, the Law of Sines is needed to find the missing angle measure. The Law of Sines is $\frac{\sin A}{a} = \frac{\sin B}{b} = \frac{\sin C}{c}$, but to solve this problem we only need $\frac{\sin A}{a} = \frac{\sin B}{b}$. By substitution, that equation becomes $\frac{\sin A}{9} = \frac{\sin 72°}{13}$. Solving for A, the equation becomes $A = \sin^{-1}\left(\frac{9 \sin 72°}{13}\right) = 41.2°$, which is approximately 41°. In Answer B, 72° was subtracted from 180°, and the resulting value was divided by 2. Answer C is the measure of $\angle C$. Answer D is the measure of $\angle A$ if the equation was incorrectly set up as $\frac{\cos A}{a} = \frac{\cos B}{b}$.

Math.Content.G.SRT.11

30. C: Since the surveyor was able to determine the distance from a given spot to the two farthest ends of the pond and determine the measure of the angle between those distance lines, the Law of Cosines can be used to find the largest distance across the pond, which we will call x. Law of Cosines is $c^2 = a^2 + b^2 - 2ab \cos(C)$. If we let $a = 186$, $b = 158$ and $c = x$, then the Law of Cosines becomes $x^2 = 186^2 + 158^2 - 2(186)(158) \cos(64°)$. This simplifies as $x^2 = 33,794.30$. Therefore, $x = 183.8$ ft. Answer A used sine instead of cosine in the formula. Answer B incorrectly used the Pythagorean Theorem as $x^2 + 158^2 = 186^2$. Answer D incorrectly used the Pythagorean Theorem as $158^2 + 186^2 = x^2$.

Math.Content.G.C.1

31. A: Since all circles can be different sizes with different radii, all circles cannot be congruent, have the same area or have the same circumference. However, since all circles maintain the same shape and the ratio Circumference/Diameter is always equal to π, all circles are similar.

Math.Content.G.C.2

32. C: In the figure, the measure of $\angle RST$ is shown to be $(3x + 9)°$. Since $\angle RST$ is inscribed in the semicircle of Circle P, as R and T are endpoints of the diameter, Thale's Theorem tells us $\angle RST$ is a right angle. Therefore, $3x + 9 = 90$. After subtracting 9 from both sides, the equation becomes $3x = 81$. Divide both sides by 3 to get $x = 27$. Answer A set up the equation as $3x + 9 = 45$. Answer B set up the equation as if the triangle were equilateral: $3x + 9 = 60$. Answer D noticed that $\angle RST$ was an inscribed angle that opened up to the semicircle, but then forgot to divide 180 by 2 to get the measure of the angle, so the equation incorrectly used was $3x + 9 = 180$.

Math.Content.G.C.3

33. C: In Circle O, $\angle ROS$ is a central angle and $\angle RTS$ is an inscribed angle. The relationship between those two types of angles is that an inscribed angle is half the measure of a central angle if they share two points on the circle. Therefore, $m\angle ROS = 2(m\angle RTS)$. By substitution, that equation becomes $16x - 4 = 2(7x+5)$. Simplifying that equation results in

$16x - 4 = 14x + 10$. After subtracting $14x$ from both sides and adding 4 to both sides, the equation becomes $2x = 14$. Divide both sides by 2 to get $x = 7$. Substituting that value for x into the expression for $m\angle RTS = 7(7) + 5 = 49 + 5 = 54°$. Answer A is the measure of $\angle RTS$ if the expressions were incorrectly set equal to each other. Answer B is the answer if the equation was correctly simplified to $16x - 4 = 14x + 10$, but then it was incorrectly simplified as $10 - 4$, instead of $10 + 4$, to get $2x = 6$. Answer D is the measure of $\angle ROS$.

Math.Content.G.C.4

34. D: Two segments that are tangent to a circle from the same point outside the circle are congruent. Therefore, $\overline{AC} \cong \overline{BC}$. By substitution, that becomes $2x + 9 = 4x - 3$. After subtracting $2x$ from both sides and adding 3 to both sides, the equation becomes $12 = 2x$. Divide both sides by 2 to get $6 = x$. To find the length of $\overline{AC}$, substitute the value for x to get $2(6) + 9 = 12 + 9 = 21$. Answer A is the value of x. Answer B is the answer if $2x + 9 = 4x - 3$ was incorrectly simplified by adding $2x$ both sides to get $12 = 6x$. Answer C is the answer if $2x + 9 = 4x - 3$ was incorrectly simplified by subtracting 3 from both sides to get $6 = 2x$.

Math.Content.G.C.5

35. A: The length of an arc intercepted by a central angle is calculated using the equation: $\frac{Central\ Angle\ Measure}{360°} \times 2\pi r$. Since the central angle measure is $48°$ and the radius is 7 cm, the equation becomes: $\frac{48°}{360°} \times 2\pi(7\ cm) = 5.9$ cm. Answer B used the diameter length instead of the radius in the calculation. Answer C is the area of sector AOB. Answer D is the circumference of the circle.

Math.Content.G.GPE.1

36. A: In order to determine the center and radius of the circle, we need to complete the square. Therefore, the equation can first be rewritten as: $x^2 + 2x + y^2 - 8y = -8$. Then, look at the x and y parts separately. For $x^2 + 2x$, we need to add $\left(\frac{2}{2}\right)^2 = (1)^2 = 1$ to both sides of the equation. For $y^2 - 8y$, we need to add $\left(\frac{-8}{2}\right)^2 = (-4)^2 = 16$ to both sides of the equation. Now, $x^2 + 2x + y^2 - 8y = -8$ becomes $x^2 + 2x + 1 + y^2 - 8y + 16 = -8 + 1 + 16$ and simplifies as $(x^2 + 2x + 1) + (y^2 - 8y + 16) = 9$. We can then factor the x and y parts separately to get $(x + 1)^2 + (y - 4)^2 = 9$. Therefore, the center of the circle is as $(-1, 4)$. The radius of the circle is the square root of 9, which is 3. In Answer B, the radius is squared and the center coordinates have the opposite signs. Answers C and D incorrectly factored the equation as $(x + 2)^2 + (y - 8)^2 = 9$, in which C took the center coordinates as $(-2, 8)$ and D took the center coordinates as $(2, -8)$.

Math.Content.G.GPE.2

37. D: Since the focus is at $(3, -3)$ and the directrix is the line $x = -5$, the vertex of the parabola is halfway between those values. Therefore, the vertex is located at $(-1, -3)$. Since the focus is located to the right of the vertex, the parabola opens to the right. A parabola that opens to the right has the general equation of $(y - k)^2 = 4p(x - h)$, where (h, k) is the vertex and the absolute value of p is the distance between the focus and the vertex and the distance between the vertex and directrix. In this problem, the focus is $(3, -3)$ and the vertex is $(-1, -3)$, so $|p| = |3 - (-1)| = |4| = 4$. Since the focus is to the right of the vertex, the value of p is positive, so $p = 4$. Substituting the values for the vertex and p into the equation, it becomes: $(y - (-3))^2 = 4(4)(x - (-1))$, $(y + 3)^2 = 16(x + 1)$. Answer A incorrectly set up the equation as $(x - h)^2 = 4p(y - k)$ and then incorrectly used the focus for (h, k) and the directrix for p. Answer B incorrectly set up the equation as $(x - h)^2 = 4p(y - k)$. Answer C correctly used the equation of $(y - k)^2 = 4p(x - h)$, but then incorrectly used the focus for (h, k) and the directrix for p.

Math.Content.G.GPE.3

38. D: Since the foci are located along the line $x = 5$, the transverse axis of the hyperbola is vertical. This means the general equation for the hyperbola is $\frac{(y-k)^2}{a^2} - \frac{(x-h)^2}{b^2} = 1$, where (h, k) is the center of the hyperbola, and a is half the difference of the distances from the foci to a point on the hyperbola. Since the center is located between the foci of $(5, -4)$ and $(5, 8)$, the center of the hyperbola is located at $(5, 2)$ and the distance from the center to each focus, c, is 6. The difference of the distances from the foci to a point on the hyperbola is equivalent to $2a$. Therefore, $2a = 10$, so $a = 5$ and $a^2 = 25$. To find the value of b^2, we use the equation $b^2 = c^2 - a^2$. Substituting in for that equation, $b^2 = 6^2 - 5^2 = 36 - 25 = 11$. Based on the center $(5, 2)$, $a^2 = 25$ and $b^2 = 11$, the equation for the hyperbola becomes $\frac{(y-2)^2}{25} - \frac{(x-5)^2}{11} = 1$. Answer C used addition instead of subtraction in the equation. Answers A and B reversed the $(x - 5)$ and $(y - 2)$ values and answer A used addition instead of subtraction.

Math.Content.G.GPE.4

39. C: First, plot the coordinate points to get an idea for the basic shape, as shown below.

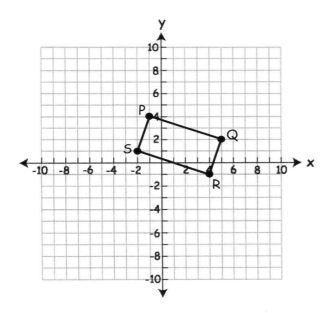

Next, use the distance formula ($d = \sqrt{(x_2 - x_1)^2 + (y_2 - y_1)^2}$) to determine the lengths of all four sides: $PQ = \sqrt{(5 - -1)^2 + (2 - 4)^2} = 6.32$, $QR = \sqrt{(4 - 5)^2 + (-1 - 2)^2} = 3.16$, $RS = \sqrt{(-2 - 4)^2 + (1 - -1)^2} = 6.32$, $SP = \sqrt{(-1 - -2)^2 + (4 - 1)^2} = 3.16$. This shows that the lengths of $PQ = RS$ and $QR = PS$. Next calculate the slopes of the four sides: Slope of $\overline{PQ} = \frac{2-4}{5-(-1)} = \frac{-2}{6} = -\frac{1}{3}$, Slope of $\overline{QR} = \frac{-1-2}{4-5} = \frac{-3}{-1} = 3$, Slope of $\overline{RS} = \frac{1-(-1)}{-2-4} = \frac{2}{-6} = -\frac{1}{3}$, Slope of $\overline{SP} = \frac{4-1}{-1-(-2)} = \frac{3}{1} = 3$. Since the slopes of $\overline{PQ}$ and $\overline{QR}$ are opposite reciprocal, it means that those segments are perpendicular and form 90°angles. Similarly, $\overline{QR}$ and $\overline{RS}$, $\overline{RS}$ and $\overline{SP}$, and $\overline{SP}$ and $\overline{PQ}$ all have opposite reciprocal slopes, so those segments are also

- 123 -

perpendicular to each other and form 90°angles. Since quadrilateral *PQRS* has four right angles and the lengths of the opposite sides of the quadrilateral are congruent, this shape is a rectangle.

Math.Content.G.GPE.5

40. B: The slope of the original line is $m = -\frac{1}{2}$. Since the new line needs to be parallel, the new line's slope will be equal to the original slope of $m = -\frac{1}{2}$. The given point is (–4, –2), which is equivalent to (x_1, y_1) in the point-slope equation of $y - y_1 = m(x - x_1)$. Substituting the slope and given point, the point-slope equation becomes $y - (-2) = -\frac{1}{2}(x - (-4))$. Simplifying this equation becomes $y + 2 = -\frac{1}{2}(x + 4)$. Distributing on the right side of the equation results in $y + 2 = -\frac{1}{2}x - 2$. Subtract 2 from both sides of the equation to get the parallel line of $y = -\frac{1}{2}x - 4$. Then, convert the point-slope form into standard form by first adding $\frac{1}{2}x$ to both sides of the equation: $\frac{1}{2}x + y = -4$. Then multiply every term by 2 to cancel out the $\frac{1}{2}$ fraction to get: $x + 2y = -8$. Answer A incorrectly set up the point-slope equation as $y - 2 = -\frac{1}{2}(x - 4)$. Answers C and D used the perpendicular (or opposite reciprocal) slope. Answer C also incorrectly set up the given points in the equation as was done in Answer A.

Math.Content.G.GPE.6

41. A: If point *T* is twice as far from *S* as it is from *R*, it means that the ratio of distance from *T* to *R* and *S* is 1:2, respectively. Therefore, the line segment can be broken up into 1 + 2 = 3 equal segments. The total distance between points *R* and *S* is 12 – 0 = 12 units. If we divide 12 by 3, each equal segment is 4 units in length. We then can multiply the ratio by 4 to get the actual distances from *T* to *R* and *S*, 1(4):2(4) = 4:8. So, *T* is located 4 units from *R* and 8 units from *S*. Since *R* is located at 0, it means that 0 + 4 = 4. Answer B is just halfway between points *R* and *S*. Answer C is the point twice as far from *R* as it is from *S*. Answer D is a point two units from *S* instead of twice as far from *S* than *R*.

Math.Content.G.GPE.7

42. D: The perimeter of $\triangle ABC$ is *AB* + *BC* + *AC*. In order to find the perimeter, we need to find the length of each side of the triangle. To do this, apply the distance formula to the sides *AB*, *BC* and *AC*. The coordinates of the triangle vertices are *A*(–6, –5), *B*(3, 5), and *C*(7, –3). The distance formula is: $d = \sqrt{(x_2 - x_1)^2 + (y_2 - y_1)^2}$. The length of side $AB = \sqrt{(3 - -6)^2 + (5 - -5)^2} = \sqrt{(9)^2 + (10)^2} = \sqrt{81 + 100} = \sqrt{181} = 13.45$. The length of side $BC = \sqrt{(7 - 3)^2 + (-3 - 5)^2} = \sqrt{(4)^2 + (-8)^2} = \sqrt{16 + 64} = \sqrt{80} = 8.94$. The length of side $AC = \sqrt{(7 - -6)^2 + (-3 - -5)^2} = \sqrt{(13)^2 + (2)^2} = \sqrt{169 + 4} = \sqrt{173} = 13.15$. Therefore, the perimeter of $\triangle ABC$ is 13.45 + 8.94 + 13.15 = 35.54 units. Answer A did not square the values after subtracting the pairs of *x* and *y* values. Answer B incorrectly set up the distance formula as $d = \sqrt{(x_2 + x_1)^2 + (y_2 + y_1)^2}$. Answer C incorrectly subtracted the smaller squared value from the larger squared value under the radical for each side.

Math.Content.G.GMD.1

43. B: When the wedges are rearranged into the rectangle, half of the wedge arcs form the top length of the rectangle and the other half of the wedge arcs form the bottom length of the rectangle. Since all of the wedge arcs combine to form the entire circumference of the circle, the length of the rectangle is half of the circumference of the circle. The formula for the circumference of a circle with radius r is $C = 2\pi r$. Half of that circumference is $\left(\frac{1}{2}\right) 2\pi r = \pi r$. Answer C is the width of the rectangle. Answer D is the area of the rectangle.

Math.Content.G.GMD.2

44. B: Cavalier's principle states that if all corresponding cross sections of two solids have the same area, then those two solids also have the same volume. Euclid's Principles states that if p is a prime number and p divides ab, then either p divides a or p divides b. The dissection argument involves breaking down a shape or solid into smaller shapes in order to determine the formula of that shape or solid. The informal limit argument deals with finding the area of a circle by having an increasing number of triangles of the same size extend from the center of the circle to the edge of the circle and then determining the area of the circle with an infinite number of triangles on the interior.

Math.Content.G.GMD.3

45. B: The volume of the pyramid is the amount of sand needed to build the pyramid. The formula for the volume of a pyramid is $V = \frac{1}{3}BH$, where B is the area of the base and H is the height of the pyramid. Since the base is a square with sides of 10 ft, the area of the base is 10 ft × 10 ft = 100 ft². The height of the pyramid is 12 ft. Therefore, by substitution, $V = \frac{1}{3}BH$ becomes $V = \frac{1}{3}(100 \text{ ft}^2)(12 \text{ ft}) = 400$ ft³. Answer A is the lateral area of the pyramid. Answer B is lateral area after forgetting to multiply by $\frac{1}{2}$ in the lateral area formula. Answer D used the volume formula of $V = BH$ instead of $V = \frac{1}{3}BH$.

Math.Content.G.GMD.3

46. A: A beach ball is the shape of a sphere and the amount of air needed to inflate each beach ball can be expressed as the volume of the beach ball. The formula for the volume of a sphere is $V = \frac{4}{3}\pi r^3$, where r is the radius of the sphere. Since each beach ball has a diameter of 12 inches, the radius is half of the diameter, or 6 inches. Therefore, by substitution, $V = \frac{4}{3}\pi r^3$ becomes $V = \frac{4}{3}\pi (6 \text{ in})^3 = 904.8$ in³. Answer B forgot to divide by 3. Answer C used the diameter instead of the radius. Answer D forgot to divide by 3 and used the diameter instead of the radius.

Math.Content.G.GMD.4

47. B: When the rectangle is rotated about the shown vertical axis, it will create circular bases along the top and bottom while still maintaining the vertical line along the sides. Therefore, the 3-D object generated will be a cylinder.

Math.Content.G.MG.1

48. B: The formula for the surface area of a sphere is $SA = 4\pi r^2$. Since the radius of Earth is 6,378.1 km, the surface area of the Earth is calculated as $SA = 4\pi(6,378.1 \text{ km})^2 = 5.11 \times 10^8$ km². Answer A incorrectly used the formula $\frac{4}{3}\pi r^2$ for the surface area. Answer C is the volume of Earth. Answer D incorrectly used the formula $4\pi r^3$ for the surface area.

Math.Content.G.MG.2

49. C: To determine the density of marbles per cubic foot, the calculation takes the number of marbles in the box divided by the volume of the box. The dimensions of the box are 3 ft×

2 ft × 6 in. Since the dimensions are not all in the same unit, 6 in is converted into 0.5 ft. The volume of the box then becomes 3 ft × 2 ft × 0.5 ft = 3 ft³. The density of marbles per cubic foot is then calculated as $\frac{5{,}184\ marbles}{3\ ft^3}$ = 1,728 marbles/cubic foot. Answer A incorrectly calculated the volume of the box by not converting 6 in into feet and multiplied 3 × 2 × 6 to get 36 ft³. Answer B incorrectly divided the number of marbles only by the area of the bottom of the box (3 ft× 2 ft). Answer D incorrectly multiplied the number of marbles by the volume of the box.

Math.Content.G.MG.3

50. C: The amount of land covered by the walkway is the difference between the area of the entire plot of land and the area of the fountain. The area of the entire plot of land is 30 ft × 30 ft = 900 ft². The area of the fountain can be found using the equation $A = \pi r^2$ since the fountain is circular. The diameter of the fountain is 16 ft, so the radius is 8 ft. Therefore, the area of the fountain is $A = \pi(8\ \text{ft})^2$ = 201.1 ft². The area of the walkway is then calculated as 900 ft² – 201.1 ft² = 698.9 ft². Answer A is the area of the walkway if the diameter of the fountain was incorrectly used to calculate the fountain area. Answer B is the area of the fountain. Answer D is the area of the plot of land.

Secret Key #1 - Time is Your Greatest Enemy

Pace Yourself

Wear a watch. At the beginning of the test, check the time (or start a chronometer on your watch to count the minutes), and check the time after every few questions to make sure you are "on schedule."

If you are forced to speed up, do it efficiently. Usually one or more answer choices can be eliminated without too much difficulty. Above all, don't panic. Don't speed up and just begin guessing at random choices. By pacing yourself, and continually monitoring your progress against your watch, you will always know exactly how far ahead or behind you are with your available time. If you find that you are one minute behind on the test, don't skip one question without spending any time on it, just to catch back up. Take 15 fewer seconds on the next four questions, and after four questions you'll have caught back up. Once you catch back up, you can continue working each problem at your normal pace.

Furthermore, don't dwell on the problems that you were rushed on. If a problem was taking up too much time and you made a hurried guess, it must be difficult. The difficult questions are the ones you are most likely to miss anyway, so it isn't a big loss. It is better to end with more time than you need than to run out of time.

Lastly, sometimes it is beneficial to slow down if you are constantly getting ahead of time. You are always more likely to catch a careless mistake by working more slowly than quickly, and among very high-scoring test takers (those who are likely to have lots of time left over), careless errors affect the score more than mastery of material.

Secret Key #2 - Guessing is not Guesswork

You probably know that guessing is a good idea. Unlike other standardized tests, there is no penalty for getting a wrong answer. Even if you have no idea about a question, you still have a 20-25% chance of getting it right.

Most test takers do not understand the impact that proper guessing can have on their score. Unless you score extremely high, guessing will significantly contribute to your final score.

Monkeys Take the Test

What most test takers don't realize is that to insure that 20-25% chance, you have to guess randomly. If you put 20 monkeys in a room to take this test, assuming they answered once per question and behaved themselves, on average they would get 20-25% of the questions correct. Put 20 test takers in the room, and the average will be much lower among guessed questions. Why?

1. The test writers intentionally write deceptive answer choices that "look" right. A test taker has no idea about a question, so he picks the "best looking" answer, which is often wrong. The monkey has no idea what looks good and what doesn't, so it will consistently be right about 20-25% of the time.
2. Test takers will eliminate answer choices from the guessing pool based on a hunch or intuition. Simple but correct answers often get excluded, leaving a 0% chance of being correct. The monkey has no clue, and often gets lucky with the best choice.

This is why the process of elimination endorsed by most test courses is flawed and detrimental to your performance. Test takers don't guess; they make an ignorant stab in the dark that is usually worse than random.

$5 Challenge

Let me introduce one of the most valuable ideas of this course—the $5 challenge:
- *You only mark your "best guess" if you are willing to bet $5 on it.*
- *You only eliminate choices from guessing if you are willing to bet $5 on it.*

Why $5? Five dollars is an amount of money that is small yet not insignificant, and can really add up fast (20 questions could cost you $100). Likewise, each answer choice on one question of the test will have a small impact on your overall score, but it can really add up to a lot of points in the end.

The process of elimination IS valuable. The following shows your chance of guessing it right:

If you eliminate wrong answer choices until only this many remain:	Chance of getting it correct:
1	100%
2	50%
3	33%

However, if you accidentally eliminate the right answer or go on a hunch for an incorrect answer, your chances drop dramatically—to 0%. By guessing among all the answer choices, you are GUARANTEED to have a shot at the right answer.

That's why the $5 test is so valuable. If you give up the advantage and safety of a pure guess, it had better be worth the risk.

What we still haven't covered is how to be sure that whatever guess you make is truly random. Here's the easiest way:
- *Always pick the first answer choice among those remaining.*

Such a technique means that you have decided, **before you see a single test question**, exactly how you are going to guess, and since the order of choices tells you nothing about which one is correct, this guessing technique is perfectly random.

This section is not meant to scare you away from making educated guesses or eliminating choices; you just need to define when a choice is worth eliminating. The $5 test, along with a pre-defined random guessing strategy, is the best way to make sure you reap all of the benefits of guessing.

Secret Key #3 - Practice Smarter, Not Harder

Many test takers delay the test preparation process because they dread the awful amounts of practice time they think necessary to succeed on the test. We have refined an effective method that will take you only a fraction of the time.

There are a number of "obstacles" in the path to success. Among these are answering questions, finishing in time, and mastering test-taking strategies. All must be executed on the day of the test at peak performance, or your score will suffer. The test is a mental marathon that has a large impact on your future.

Just like a marathon runner, it is important to work your way up to the full challenge. So first you just worry about questions, and then time, and finally strategy:

Success Strategy

1. Find a good source for practice tests.
2. If you are willing to make a larger time investment, consider using more than one study guide. Often the different approaches of multiple authors will help you "get" difficult concepts.
3. Take a practice test with no time constraints, with all study helps, "open book." Take your time with questions and focus on applying strategies.
4. Take a practice test with time constraints, with all guides, "open book."
5. Take a final practice test without open material and with time limits.

If you have time to take more practice tests, just repeat step 5. By gradually exposing yourself to the full rigors of the test environment, you will condition your mind to the stress of test day and maximize your success.

Secret Key #4 - Prepare, Don't Procrastinate

Let me state an obvious fact: if you take the test three times, you will probably get three different scores. This is due to the way you feel on test day, the level of preparedness you have, and the version of the test you see. Despite the test writers' claims to the contrary, some versions of the test WILL be easier for you than others.

Since your future depends so much on your score, you should maximize your chances of success. In order to maximize the likelihood of success, you've got to prepare in advance. This means taking practice tests and spending time learning the information and test taking strategies you will need to succeed.

Never go take the actual test as a "practice" test, expecting that you can just take it again if you need to. Take all the practice tests you can on your own, but when you go to take the official test, be prepared, be focused, and do your best the first time!

Secret Key #5 - Test Yourself

Everyone knows that time is money. There is no need to spend too much of your time or too little of your time preparing for the test. You should only spend as much of your precious time preparing as is necessary for you to get the score you need.

Once you have taken a practice test under real conditions of time constraints, then you will know if you are ready for the test or not.

If you have scored extremely high the first time that you take the practice test, then there is not much point in spending countless hours studying. You are already there.

Benchmark your abilities by retaking practice tests and seeing how much you have improved. Once you consistently score high enough to guarantee success, then you are ready.

If you have scored well below where you need, then knuckle down and begin studying in earnest. Check your improvement regularly through the use of practice tests under real conditions. Above all, don't worry, panic, or give up. The key is perseverance!

Then, when you go to take the test, remain confident and remember how well you did on the practice tests. If you can score high enough on a practice test, then you can do the same on the real thing.

General Strategies

The most important thing you can do is to ignore your fears and jump into the test immediately. Do not be overwhelmed by any strange-sounding terms. You have to jump into the test like jumping into a pool—all at once is the easiest way.

Make Predictions

As you read and understand the question, try to guess what the answer will be. Remember that several of the answer choices are wrong, and once you begin reading them, your mind will immediately become cluttered with answer choices designed to throw you off. Your mind is typically the most focused immediately after you have read the question and digested its contents. If you can, try to predict what the correct answer will be. You may be surprised at what you can predict.

Quickly scan the choices and see if your prediction is in the listed answer choices. If it is, then you can be quite confident that you have the right answer. It still won't hurt to check the other answer choices, but most of the time, you've got it!

Answer the Question

It may seem obvious to only pick answer choices that answer the question, but the test writers can create some excellent answer choices that are wrong. Don't pick an answer just because it sounds right, or you believe it to be true. It MUST answer the question. Once you've made your selection, always go back and check it against the question and make sure that you didn't misread the question and that the answer choice does answer the question posed.

Benchmark

After you read the first answer choice, decide if you think it sounds correct or not. If it doesn't, move on to the next answer choice. If it does, mentally mark that answer choice. This doesn't mean that you've definitely selected it as your answer choice, it just means that it's the best you've seen thus far. Go ahead and read the next choice. If the next choice is worse than the one you've already selected, keep going to the next answer choice. If the next choice is better than the choice you've already selected, mentally mark the new answer choice as your best guess.The first answer choice that you select becomes your standard. Every other answer choice must be benchmarked against that standard. That choice is correct until proven otherwise by another answer choice beating it out. Once you've decided that no other answer choice seems as good, do one final check to ensure that your answer choice answers the question posed.

Valid Information

Don't discount any of the information provided in the question. Every piece of information may be necessary to determine the correct answer. None of the information in the question is there to throw you off (while the answer choices will certainly have information to throw you off). If two seemingly unrelated topics are discussed, don't ignore either. You can be confident there is a relationship, or it wouldn't be included in the question, and you are probably going to have to determine what is that relationship to find the answer.

Avoid "Fact Traps"

Don't get distracted by a choice that is factually true. Your search is for the answer that answers the question. Stay focused and don't fall for an answer that is true but irrelevant. Always go back to the question and make sure you're choosing an answer that actually answers the question and is not just a true statement. An answer can be factually correct, but it MUST answer the question asked. Additionally, two answers can both be seemingly correct, so be sure to read all of the answer choices, and make sure that you get the one that BEST answers the question.

Milk the Question

Some of the questions may throw you completely off. They might deal with a subject you have not been exposed to, or one that you haven't reviewed in years. While your lack of knowledge about the subject will be a hindrance, the question itself can give you many clues that will help you find the correct answer. Read the question carefully and look for clues. Watch particularly for adjectives and nouns describing difficult terms or words that you don't recognize. Regardless of whether you completely understand a word or not, replacing it with a synonym, either provided or one you more familiar with, may help you to understand what the questions are asking. Rather than wracking your mind about specific detailed information concerning a difficult term or word, try to use mental substitutes that are easier to understand.

The Trap of Familiarity

Don't just choose a word because you recognize it. On difficult questions, you may not recognize a number of words in the answer choices. The test writers don't put "make-believe" words on the test, so don't think that just because you only recognize all the words in one answer choice that that answer choice must be correct. If you only recognize words in one answer choice, then focus on that one. Is it correct? Try your best to determine if it is correct. If it is, that's great. If not, eliminate it. Each word and answer choice you eliminate increases your chances of getting the question correct, even if you then have to guess among the unfamiliar choices.

Eliminate Answers

Eliminate choices as soon as you realize they are wrong. But be careful! Make sure you consider all of the possible answer choices. Just because one appears right, doesn't mean that the next one won't be even better! The test writers will usually put more than one good answer choice for every question, so read all of them. Don't worry if you are stuck between two that seem right. By getting down to just two remaining possible choices, your odds are now 50/50. Rather than wasting too much time, play the odds. You are guessing, but guessing wisely because you've been able to knock out some of the answer choices that you know are wrong. If you are eliminating choices and realize that the last answer choice you are left with is also obviously wrong, don't panic. Start over and consider each choice again. There may easily be something that you missed the first time and will realize on the second pass.

Tough Questions

If you are stumped on a problem or it appears too hard or too difficult, don't waste time. Move on! Remember though, if you can quickly check for obviously incorrect answer choices, your chances of guessing correctly are greatly improved. Before you completely give up, at least try to knock out a couple of possible answers. Eliminate what you can and then guess at the remaining answer choices before moving on.

Brainstorm

If you get stuck on a difficult question, spend a few seconds quickly brainstorming. Run through the complete list of possible answer choices. Look at each choice and ask yourself, "Could this answer the question satisfactorily?" Go through each answer choice and consider it independently of the others. By systematically going through all possibilities, you may find something that you would otherwise overlook. Remember though that when you get stuck, it's important to try to keep moving.

Read Carefully

Understand the problem. Read the question and answer choices carefully. Don't miss the question because you misread the terms. You have plenty of time to read each question thoroughly and make sure you understand what is being asked. Yet a happy medium must be attained, so don't waste too much time. You must read carefully, but efficiently.

Face Value

When in doubt, use common sense. Always accept the situation in the problem at face value. Don't read too much into it. These problems will not require you to make huge leaps of logic. The test writers aren't trying to throw you off with a cheap trick. If you have to go beyond creativity and make a leap of logic in order to have an answer choice answer the question, then you should look at the other answer choices. Don't overcomplicate the problem by creating theoretical relationships or explanations that will warp time or space. These are normal problems rooted in reality. It's just that the applicable relationship or explanation may not be readily apparent and you have to figure things out. Use your common sense to interpret anything that isn't clear.

Prefixes

If you're having trouble with a word in the question or answer choices, try dissecting it. Take advantage of every clue that the word might include. Prefixes and suffixes can be a huge help. Usually they allow you to determine a basic meaning. Pre- means before, post- means after, pro - is positive, de- is negative. From these prefixes and suffixes, you can get an idea of the general meaning of the word and try to put it into context. Beware though of any traps. Just because con- is the opposite of pro-, doesn't necessarily mean congress is the opposite of progress!

Hedge Phrases

Watch out for critical hedge phrases, led off with words such as "likely," "may," "can," "sometimes," "often," "almost," "mostly," "usually," "generally," "rarely," and "sometimes." Question writers insert these hedge phrases to cover every possibility. Often an answer choice will be wrong simply because it leaves no room for exception. Unless the situation calls for them, avoid answer choices that have definitive words like "exactly," and "always."

Switchback Words

Stay alert for "switchbacks." These are the words and phrases frequently used to alert you to shifts in thought. The most common switchback word is "but." Others include "although," "however," "nevertheless," "on the other hand," "even though," "while," "in spite of," "despite," and "regardless of."

New Information

Correct answer choices will rarely have completely new information included. Answer choices typically are straightforward reflections of the material asked about and will directly relate to the question. If a new piece of information is included in an answer choice that doesn't even seem to relate to the topic being asked about, then that answer choice is likely incorrect. All of the information needed to answer the question is usually provided for you in the question. You should not have to make guesses that are unsupported or choose answer choices that require unknown information that cannot be reasoned from what is given.

Time Management

On technical questions, don't get lost on the technical terms. Don't spend too much time on any one question. If you don't know what a term means, then odds are you aren't going to get much further since you don't have a dictionary. You should be able to immediately recognize whether or not you know a term. If you don't, work with the other clues that you have—the other answer choices and terms provided—but don't waste too much time trying to figure out a difficult term that you don't know.

Contextual Clues

Look for contextual clues. An answer can be right but not the correct answer. The contextual clues will help you find the answer that is most right and is correct. Understand the context in which a phrase or statement is made. This will help you make important distinctions.

Don't Panic

Panicking will not answer any questions for you; therefore, it isn't helpful. When you first see the question, if your mind goes blank, take a deep breath. Force yourself to mechanically go through the steps of solving the problem using the strategies you've learned.

Pace Yourself

Don't get clock fever. It's easy to be overwhelmed when you're looking at a page full of questions, your mind is full of random thoughts and feeling confused, and the clock is ticking down faster than you would like. Calm down and maintain the pace that you have set for yourself. As long as you are on track by monitoring your pace, you are guaranteed to have enough time for yourself. When you get to the last few minutes of the test, it may seem like you won't have enough time left, but if you only have as many questions as you should have left at that point, then you're right on track!

Answer Selection

The best way to pick an answer choice is to eliminate all of those that are wrong, until only one is left and confirm that is the correct answer. Sometimes though, an answer choice may immediately look right. Be careful! Take a second to make sure that the other choices are not equally obvious. Don't make a hasty mistake. There are only two times that you should stop before checking other answers. First is when you are positive that the answer choice you have selected is correct. Second is when time is almost out and you have to make a quick guess!

Check Your Work

Since you will probably not know every term listed and the answer to every question, it is important that you get credit for the ones that you do know. Don't miss any questions through careless mistakes. If at all possible, try to take a second to look back over your answer selection and make sure you've selected the correct answer choice and haven't made a costly careless mistake (such as marking an answer choice that you didn't mean to mark). The time it takes for this quick double check should more than pay for itself in caught mistakes.

Beware of Directly Quoted Answers

Sometimes an answer choice will repeat word for word a portion of the question or reference section. However, beware of such exact duplication. It may be a trap! More than likely, the correct choice will paraphrase or summarize a point, rather than being exactly the same wording.

Slang

Scientific sounding answers are better than slang ones. An answer choice that begins "To compare the outcomes…" is much more likely to be correct than one that begins "Because some people insisted…"

Extreme Statements

Avoid wild answers that throw out highly controversial ideas that are proclaimed as established fact. An answer choice that states the "process should used in certain situations, if…" is much more likely to be correct than one that states the "process should be discontinued completely." The first is a calm rational statement and doesn't even make a definitive, uncompromising stance, using a hedge word "if" to provide wiggle room, whereas the second choice is a radical idea and far more extreme.

Answer Choice Families

When you have two or more answer choices that are direct opposites or parallels, one of them is usually the correct answer. For instance, if one answer choice states "x increases" and another answer choice states "x decreases" or "y increases," then those two or three answer choices are very similar in construction and fall into the same family of answer choices. A family of answer choices consists of two or three answer choices, very similar in construction, but often with directly opposite meanings. Usually the correct answer choice will be in that family of answer choices. The "odd man out" or answer choice that doesn't seem to fit the parallel construction of the other answer choices is more likely to be incorrect.

Special Report: How to Overcome Test Anxiety

The very nature of tests caters to some level of anxiety, nervousness, or tension, just as we feel for any important event that occurs in our lives. A little bit of anxiety or nervousness can be a good thing. It helps us with motivation, and makes achievement just that much sweeter. However, too much anxiety can be a problem, especially if it hinders our ability to function and perform.

"Test anxiety," is the term that refers to the emotional reactions that some test-takers experience when faced with a test or exam. Having a fear of testing and exams is based upon a rational fear, since the test-taker's performance can shape the course of an academic career. Nevertheless, experiencing excessive fear of examinations will only interfere with the test-taker's ability to perform and chance to be successful.

There are a large variety of causes that can contribute to the development and sensation of test anxiety. These include, but are not limited to, lack of preparation and worrying about issues surrounding the test.

Lack of Preparation

Lack of preparation can be identified by the following behaviors or situations:
- Not scheduling enough time to study, and therefore cramming the night before the test or exam
- Managing time poorly, to create the sensation that there is not enough time to do everything
- Failing to organize the text information in advance, so that the study material consists of the entire text and not simply the pertinent information
- Poor overall studying habits

Worrying, on the other hand, can be related to both the test taker, or many other factors around him/her that will be affected by the results of the test. These include worrying about:
- Previous performances on similar exams, or exams in general
- How friends and other students are achieving
- The negative consequences that will result from a poor grade or failure

There are three primary elements to test anxiety. Physical components, which involve the same typical bodily reactions as those to acute anxiety (to be discussed below). Emotional factors have to do with fear or panic. Mental or cognitive issues concerning attention spans and memory abilities.

Physical Signals

There are many different symptoms of test anxiety, and these are not limited to mental and emotional strain. Frequently there are a range of physical signals that will let a test taker know that he/she is suffering from test anxiety. These bodily changes can include the following:

- Perspiring
- Sweaty palms
- Wet, trembling hands
- Nausea
- Dry mouth
- A knot in the stomach
- Headache
- Faintness
- Muscle tension
- Aching shoulders, back and neck
- Rapid heart beat
- Feeling too hot/cold

To recognize the sensation of test anxiety, a test-taker should monitor him/herself for the following sensations:

- The physical distress symptoms as listed above
- Emotional sensitivity, expressing emotional feelings such as the need to cry or laugh too much, or a sensation of anger or helplessness
- A decreased ability to think, causing the test-taker to blank out or have racing thoughts that are hard to organize or control.

Though most students will feel some level of anxiety when faced with a test or exam, the majority can cope with that anxiety and maintain it at a manageable level. However, those who cannot are faced with a very real and very serious condition, which can and should be controlled for the immeasurable benefit of this sufferer.

Naturally, these sensations lead to negative results for the testing experience. The most common effects of test anxiety have to do with nervousness and mental blocking.

Nervousness

Nervousness can appear in several different levels:

- The test-taker's difficulty, or even inability to read and understand the questions on the test
- The difficulty or inability to organize thoughts to a coherent form
- The difficulty or inability to recall key words and concepts relating to the testing questions (especially essays)
- The receipt of poor grades on a test, though the test material was well known by the test taker

Conversely, a person may also experience mental blocking, which involves:
- Blanking out on test questions
- Only remembering the correct answers to the questions when the test has already finished.

Fortunately for test anxiety sufferers, beating these feelings, to a large degree, has to do with proper preparation. When a test taker has a feeling of preparedness, then anxiety will be dramatically lessened.

The first step to resolving anxiety issues is to distinguish which of the two types of anxiety are being suffered. If the anxiety is a direct result of a lack of preparation, this should be considered a normal reaction, and the anxiety level (as opposed to the test results) shouldn't be anything to worry about. However, if, when adequately prepared, the test-taker still panics, blanks out, or seems to overreact, this is not a fully rational reaction. While this can be considered normal too, there are many ways to combat and overcome these effects.

Remember that anxiety cannot be entirely eliminated, however, there are ways to minimize it, to make the anxiety easier to manage. Preparation is one of the best ways to minimize test anxiety. Therefore the following techniques are wise in order to best fight off any anxiety that may want to build.

To begin with, try to avoid cramming before a test, whenever it is possible. By trying to memorize an entire term's worth of information in one day, you'll be shocking your system, and not giving yourself a very good chance to absorb the information. This is an easy path to anxiety, so for those who suffer from test anxiety, cramming should not even be considered an option.

Instead of cramming, work throughout the semester to combine all of the material which is presented throughout the semester, and work on it gradually as the course goes by, making sure to master the main concepts first, leaving minor details for a week or so before the test.

To study for the upcoming exam, be sure to pose questions that may be on the examination, to gauge the ability to answer them by integrating the ideas from your texts, notes and lectures, as well as any supplementary readings.

If it is truly impossible to cover all of the information that was covered in that particular term, concentrate on the most important portions, that can be covered very well. Learn these concepts as best as possible, so that when the test comes, a goal can be made to use these concepts as presentations of your knowledge.

In addition to study habits, changes in attitude are critical to beating a struggle with test anxiety. In fact, an improvement of the perspective over the entire test-taking experience can actually help a test taker to enjoy studying and therefore improve the overall experience. Be certain not to overemphasize the significance of the grade - know that the result of the test is neither a reflection of self worth, nor is it a measure of intelligence; one grade will not predict a person's future success.

To improve an overall testing outlook, the following steps should be tried:
- Keeping in mind that the most reasonable expectation for taking a test is to expect to try to demonstrate as much of what you know as you possibly can.
- Reminding ourselves that a test is only one test; this is not the only one, and there will be others.
- The thought of thinking of oneself in an irrational, all-or-nothing term should be avoided at all costs.
- A reward should be designated for after the test, so there's something to look forward to. Whether it be going to a movie, going out to eat, or simply visiting friends, schedule it in advance, and do it no matter what result is expected on the exam.

Test-takers should also keep in mind that the basics are some of the most important things, even beyond anti-anxiety techniques and studying. Never neglect the basic social, emotional and biological needs, in order to try to absorb information. In order to best achieve, these three factors must be held as just as important as the studying itself.

Study Steps

Remember the following important steps for studying:
- Maintain healthy nutrition and exercise habits. Continue both your recreational activities and social pass times. These both contribute to your physical and emotional well being.
- Be certain to get a good amount of sleep, especially the night before the test, because when you're overtired you are not able to perform to the best of your best ability.
- Keep the studying pace to a moderate level by taking breaks when they are needed, and varying the work whenever possible, to keep the mind fresh instead of getting bored.
- When enough studying has been done that all the material that can be learned has been learned, and the test taker is prepared for the test, stop studying and do something relaxing such as listening to music, watching a movie, or taking a warm bubble bath.

There are also many other techniques to minimize the uneasiness or apprehension that is experienced along with test anxiety before, during, or even after the examination. In fact, there are a great deal of things that can be done to stop anxiety from interfering with lifestyle and performance. Again, remember that anxiety will not be eliminated entirely, and it shouldn't be. Otherwise that "up" feeling for exams would not exist, and most of us depend on that sensation to perform better than usual. However, this anxiety has to be at a level that is manageable.

Of course, as we have just discussed, being prepared for the exam is half the battle right away. Attending all classes, finding out what knowledge will be expected on the exam, and knowing the exam schedules are easy steps to lowering anxiety. Keeping up with work will remove the need to cram, and efficient study habits will eliminate wasted time. Studying should be done in an ideal location for concentration, so that it is simple to become interested in the material and give it complete attention. A method such as

SQ3R (Survey, Question, Read, Recite, Review) is a wonderful key to follow to make sure that the study habits are as effective as possible, especially in the case of learning from a textbook. Flashcards are great techniques for memorization. Learning to take good notes will mean that notes will be full of useful information, so that less sifting will need to be done to seek out what is pertinent for studying. Reviewing notes after class and then again on occasion will keep the information fresh in the mind. From notes that have been taken summary sheets and outlines can be made for simpler reviewing.

A study group can also be a very motivational and helpful place to study, as there will be a sharing of ideas, all of the minds can work together, to make sure that everyone understands, and the studying will be made more interesting because it will be a social occasion. Basically, though, as long as the test-taker remains organized and self confident, with efficient study habits, less time will need to be spent studying, and higher grades will be achieved.

To become self confident, there are many useful steps. The first of these is "self talk." It has been shown through extensive research, that self-talk for students who suffer from test anxiety, should be well monitored, in order to make sure that it contributes to self confidence as opposed to sinking the student. Frequently the self talk of test-anxious students is negative or self-defeating, thinking that everyone else is smarter and faster, that they always mess up, and that if they don't do well, they'll fail the entire course. It is important to decreasing anxiety that awareness is made of self talk. Try writing any negative self thoughts and then disputing them with a positive statement instead. Begin self-encouragement as though it was a friend speaking. Repeat positive statements to help reprogram the mind to believing in successes instead of failures.

Helpful Techniques

Other extremely helpful techniques include:
- Self-visualization of doing well and reaching goals
- While aiming for an "A" level of understanding, don't try to "overprotect" by setting your expectations lower. This will only convince the mind to stop studying in order to meet the lower expectations.
- Don't make comparisons with the results or habits of other students. These are individual factors, and different things work for different people, causing different results.
- Strive to become an expert in learning what works well, and what can be done in order to improve. Consider collecting this data in a journal.
- Create rewards for after studying instead of doing things before studying that will only turn into avoidance behaviors.
- Make a practice of relaxing - by using methods such as progressive relaxation, self-hypnosis, guided imagery, etc - in order to make relaxation an automatic sensation.
- Work on creating a state of relaxed concentration so that concentrating will take on the focus of the mind, so that none will be wasted on worrying.
- Take good care of the physical self by eating well and getting enough sleep.
- Plan in time for exercise and stick to this plan.

Beyond these techniques, there are other methods to be used before, during and after the test that will help the test-taker perform well in addition to overcoming anxiety.

Before the exam comes the academic preparation. This involves establishing a study schedule and beginning at least one week before the actual date of the test. By doing this, the anxiety of not having enough time to study for the test will be automatically eliminated. Moreover, this will make the studying a much more effective experience, ensuring that the learning will be an easier process. This relieves much undue pressure on the test-taker.

Summary sheets, note cards, and flash cards with the main concepts and examples of these main concepts should be prepared in advance of the actual studying time. A topic should never be eliminated from this process. By omitting a topic because it isn't expected to be on the test is only setting up the test-taker for anxiety should it actually appear on the exam. Utilize the course syllabus for laying out the topics that should be studied. Carefully go over the notes that were made in class, paying special attention to any of the issues that the professor took special care to emphasize while lecturing in class. In the textbooks, use the chapter review, or if possible, the chapter tests, to begin your review.

It may even be possible to ask the instructor what information will be covered on the exam, or what the format of the exam will be (for example, multiple choice, essay, free form, true-false). Additionally, see if it is possible to find out how many questions will be on the test. If a review sheet or sample test has been offered by the professor, make good use of it, above anything else, for the preparation for the test. Another great resource for getting to know the examination is reviewing tests from previous semesters. Use these tests to review, and aim to achieve a 100% score on each of the possible topics. With a few exceptions, the goal that you set for yourself is the highest one that you will reach.

Take all of the questions that were assigned as homework, and rework them to any other possible course material. The more problems reworked, the more skill and confidence will form as a result. When forming the solution to a problem, write out each of the steps. Don't simply do head work. By doing as many steps on paper as possible, much clarification and therefore confidence will be formed. Do this with as many homework problems as possible, before checking the answers. By checking the answer after each problem, a reinforcement will exist, that will not be on the exam. Study situations should be as exam-like as possible, to prime the test-taker's system for the experience. By waiting to check the answers at the end, a psychological advantage will be formed, to decrease the stress factor.

Another fantastic reason for not cramming is the avoidance of confusion in concepts, especially when it comes to mathematics. 8-10 hours of study will become one hundred percent more effective if it is spread out over a week or at least several days, instead of doing it all in one sitting. Recognize that the human brain requires time in order to assimilate new material, so frequent breaks and a span of study time over several days will be much more beneficial.

Additionally, don't study right up until the point of the exam. Studying should stop a minimum of one hour before the exam begins. This allows the brain to rest and put things in their proper order. This will also provide the time to become as relaxed as possible when going into the examination room. The test-taker will also have time to eat well and eat sensibly. Know that the brain needs food as much as the rest of the body. With enough food and enough sleep, as well as a relaxed attitude, the body and the mind are primed for success.

Avoid any anxious classmates who are talking about the exam. These students only spread anxiety, and are not worth sharing the anxious sentimentalities.

Before the test also involves creating a positive attitude, so mental preparation should also be a point of concentration. There are many keys to creating a positive attitude. Should fears become rushing in, make a visualization of taking the exam, doing well, and seeing an A written on the paper. Write out a list of affirmations that will bring a feeling of confidence, such as "I am doing well in my English class," "I studied well and know my material," "I enjoy this class." Even if the affirmations aren't believed at first, it sends a positive message to the subconscious which will result in an alteration of the overall belief system, which is the system that creates reality.

If a sensation of panic begins, work with the fear and imagine the very worst! Work through the entire scenario of not passing the test, failing the entire course, and dropping out of school, followed by not getting a job, and pushing a shopping cart through the dark alley where you'll live. This will place things into perspective! Then, practice deep breathing and create a visualization of the opposite situation - achieving an "A" on the exam, passing the entire course, receiving the degree at a graduation ceremony.

On the day of the test, there are many things to be done to ensure the best results, as well as the most calm outlook. The following stages are suggested in order to maximize test-taking potential:
- Begin the examination day with a moderate breakfast, and avoid any coffee or beverages with caffeine if the test taker is prone to jitters. Even people who are used to managing caffeine can feel jittery or light-headed when it is taken on a test day.
- Attempt to do something that is relaxing before the examination begins. As last minute cramming clouds the mastering of overall concepts, it is better to use this time to create a calming outlook.
- Be certain to arrive at the test location well in advance, in order to provide time to select a location that is away from doors, windows and other distractions, as well as giving enough time to relax before the test begins.
- Keep away from anxiety generating classmates who will upset the sensation of stability and relaxation that is being attempted before the exam.
- Should the waiting period before the exam begins cause anxiety, create a self-distraction by reading a light magazine or something else that is relaxing and simple.

During the exam itself, read the entire exam from beginning to end, and find out how much time should be allotted to each individual problem. Once writing the exam, should more time be taken for a problem, it should be abandoned, in order to begin another problem. If there is time at the end, the unfinished problem can always be returned to and completed.

Read the instructions very carefully - twice - so that unpleasant surprises won't follow during or after the exam has ended.

When writing the exam, pretend that the situation is actually simply the completion of homework within a library, or at home. This will assist in forming a relaxed atmosphere, and will allow the brain extra focus for the complex thinking function.

Begin the exam with all of the questions with which the most confidence is felt. This will build the confidence level regarding the entire exam and will begin a quality momentum. This will also create encouragement for trying the problems where uncertainty resides.

Going with the "gut instinct" is always the way to go when solving a problem. Second guessing should be avoided at all costs. Have confidence in the ability to do well.

For essay questions, create an outline in advance that will keep the mind organized and make certain that all of the points are remembered. For multiple choice, read every answer, even if the correct one has been spotted - a better one may exist.

Continue at a pace that is reasonable and not rushed, in order to be able to work carefully. Provide enough time to go over the answers at the end, to check for small errors that can be corrected.

Should a feeling of panic begin, breathe deeply, and think of the feeling of the body releasing sand through its pores. Visualize a calm, peaceful place, and include all of the sights, sounds and sensations of this image. Continue the deep breathing, and take a few minutes to continue this with closed eyes. When all is well again, return to the test.

If a "blanking" occurs for a certain question, skip it and move on to the next question. There will be time to return to the other question later. Get everything done that can be done, first, to guarantee all the grades that can be compiled, and to build all of the confidence possible. Then return to the weaker questions to build the marks from there.

Remember, one's own reality can be created, so as long as the belief is there, success will follow. And remember: anxiety can happen later, right now, there's an exam to be written!

After the examination is complete, whether there is a feeling for a good grade or a bad grade, don't dwell on the exam, and be certain to follow through on the reward that was promised...and enjoy it! Don't dwell on any mistakes that have been made, as there is nothing that can be done at this point anyway.

Additionally, don't begin to study for the next test right away. Do something relaxing for a while, and let the mind relax and prepare itself to begin absorbing information again.

From the results of the exam - both the grade and the entire experience, be certain to learn from what has gone on. Perfect studying habits and work some more on confidence in order to make the next examination experience even better than the last one.

Learn to avoid places where openings occurred for laziness, procrastination and day dreaming.

Use the time between this exam and the next one to better learn to relax, even learning to relax on cue, so that any anxiety can be controlled during the next exam. Learn how to relax the body. Slouch in your chair if that helps. Tighten and then relax all of the different muscle groups, one group at a time, beginning with the feet and then working all the way up to the neck and face. This will ultimately relax the muscles more than they were to begin with. Learn how to breathe deeply and comfortably, and focus on this breathing going in and out as a relaxing thought. With every exhale, repeat the word "relax."

As common as test anxiety is, it is very possible to overcome it. Make yourself one of the test-takers who overcome this frustrating hindrance.

Additional Bonus Material

Due to our efforts to try to keep this book to a manageable length, we've created a link that will give you access to all of your additional bonus material.

Please visit http://www.mometrix.com/bonus948/cchsgeometry to access the information.